Retrato del autor en traje de viaje

61

1. The Compleat Explorer (item 141)

Europeans in Latin America

Humboldt to Hudson

Catalogue of an exhibition
held in the Bodleian Library
December 1980 - April 1981
Prepared by
R. A. McNeil & M. D. Deas

Bodleian Library
Oxford
1980

FOREWORD

It is with pleasure, and some diffidence, that the Bodleian Library offers its first major exhibition of materials on Latin America. Diffidence, because the Library has been collecting intensively in this field for only the last fifteen years or so; pleasure because we believe this to be an excellent exhibition drawn from our holdings, the most extensive in the country outside the British Library.

The theme of the exhibition is 'Europeans in Latin America: Humboldt to Hudson' – the interaction of people from this continent with the southern part of the Americas, chiefly in the nineteenth century (and a little longer at both ends of the period). 1980 is the sesquicentennial of the death of Simón Bolívar, who stands at the centre of the heroic part of the period, and Europeans were certainly much involved in those enterprises. But Europeans were also greatly involved in other concerns – the exhibition shows explorers, scientists and naturalists, historians, men of letters among others – and how does one classify Sir Richard Burton or Roger Casement?

We hope that this exploratory exhibition will whet the appetites of those who visit it.

E.R.S.F.
2 ix 80

CONTENTS

LIST OF PLATES

The cover is adapted from the design by Johann Moritz Rugendas for *Mexico and the Mexicans*, by C. Sartorius (London, 1859).

INTRODUCTION

This exhibition has been assembled to give some idea of the richness of the Bodleian's collections on Latin America from the eighteenth to the early twentieth century, from Alexander von Humboldt to William Henry Hudson. Though the theme is broader than usual in a Bodleian exhibition, it is still far from covering the full range of the Library's holdings on Iberian America. We have included no Mexican codices – only the magnificent work on them that bankrupted Lord Kingsborough. We show no early chronicles of the Conquest, no early New World imprints, though the Bodleian is rich in these. With a few exceptions, we have not put out books *from* Latin America published in the period covered by the exhibition.

The exclusion of so much interesting material is not made only for coherence of theme and reasons of space. We wished to place the emphasis on more recent history, where the expansion of interest in Latin America within the University in the last fifteen years has been most marked. We hope also to show the strength of the Library, and our good fortune, in an area which received no systematic attention before the mid-sixties. Since then some surprising finds have been made – the fragment of Pizarro's standard, a manuscript of Nuñez de Pineda y Bascuñán's 'happy captivity' among the Araucanian Indians of Chile, a collection of nearly two thousand Mexican pamphlets from the time of independence hiding under a single general catalogue entry. Such finds are still being made: it was while preparing this exhibition that we discovered that our copy of Alcedo's *Diccionario geográfico-historico* came from the library of the Venezuelan patriot and bibliophile Francisco de Miranda.

Most of the books that the Bodleian acquired in the years covered by the exhibition were from Europe. We have chosen exhibits from the last years of colonial Spanish America and Brazil; from the monumental production of Humboldt, and from later naturalists and travellers; from the mercenaries and adventurers who fought in the wars of independence; from artists, historians and anthropologists. We have devoted cases to the Mexican Empire of Maximilian, to the Paraguayan War, to the sources of Joseph Conrad's *Nostromo* and to Roger Casement and the Putumayo atrocities. We end with some of the works of the American-Argentine-Englishman W. H. Hudson, whose *Far away and long ago* is the finest evocation of South American life in our literature, and the tribute to him from his and Conrad's friend, R.B. Cunninghame Graham.

R.A.M.
M.D.D.
8 ix 80

I THE EIGHTEENTH-CENTURY BACKGROUND

At the end of the eighteenth century, virtually all of Central and South America was ruled, as it had been for centuries, from the Iberian Peninsula: Brazil from Lisbon, and almost all the remainder from Madrid. Conquered and colonised between 1500 and 1550, the two great Spanish viceroyalties of New Spain (Mexico) and Peru had been increasingly left to their own devices throughout Spain's seventeenth-century decline. But after the establishment of Bourbon kings in Madrid, and the consequent increase of French influence, Spain made strenuous efforts to reform and revitalize her American empire. Under Philip V (king from 1700 to 1746), Ferdinand VI (1746–1759) and, especially, Charles III (1759–1788), South America was subject to a new, reforming imperialism. Two more viceroyalties were created, in the River Plate area and New Granada; defence was reorganized and commerce revived through the application of stricter, more centralized, control. (A similar reorganization was carried out in Brazil by the reforms of the Marquês do Pombal). In addition, certain scientists and explorers were welcomed to the Spanish and Portuguese Indies, and the subcontinent began once again to enter the European consciousness.

1. JORGE JUAN & ANTONIO DE ULLOA. *Relacion histórica del viaje a la América meridional hecho . . . para medir algunos grados del meridiano terrestre.* Madrid, 1748.

In 1735 the French Académie des Sciences determined to dispatch two parties to measure arcs of the meridian – one near the pole, and one near the equator. Juan and Ulloa were Spanish naval officers sent by the court in Madrid to accompany the second party, which was to do its work near Quito in the viceroyalty of Peru. The task took eight years to complete from the expedition's arrival at Quito in 1736; four years after their return to Europe this report – almost entirely the work of Ulloa – was published, to wide acclaim. Court favour ensured the volumes' wide distribution, both as a major contribution to scientific research and as a fine example of Spanish book-production – though the engravings were made in Paris. The map shown represents the complicated triangulations used to measure the line of longitude. *203 h. 190–193*

1

2. JORGE JUAN & ANTONIO DE ULLOA. *Noticias secretas de América, sobre el estado naval, militar y política de los Reynos del Peru . . . sacadas á luz por David Barry*. London, 1826.

On their return from the Quito expedition, Juan and Ulloa were instructed to prepare a second, confidential report on the political and social conditions of the viceroyalty of Peru, and on its military and naval preparedness. The report was submitted in 1748 or 1749, but as it contained frank revelations of the venality of colonial officials, the exploitation of the Indians and the dangerous antagonisms existing between Creoles and European-born Spaniards, it remained secret for nearly eighty years. At last David Barry, an English merchant trading in Cadiz, somehow obtained a copy and published it in London – at a time when Spain had just lost all control of mainland America. *Arch. Seld. A. IV. 16*

CHARLES MARIE DE LA CONDAMINE. *Journal faite par ordre du Roi à l'Equateur, servant d'introduction historique à la mesure des trois premiers degrès du méridien.* Paris, 1751.

The mathematician La Condamine had set out for Quito in 1735 with the rest of the French expedition, but he lost patience before the work was completed, and parted from his fellow-scientists in 1743. Rather than return to Europe the way he came, La Condamine decided to cross the mainland of South America, and in doing so he became the first to carry out a scientific exploration of the course of the River Amazon. The account of his travels appeared in 1745 in the *Mémoires* of the Académie des Sciences, and six years later in book form. The map shows La Condamine's routes to and from the New World, and the engraving opposite gives some idea of the conditions under which the scientists had to carry out their work of measurement. *18422 d. 11*

4. GUILLAUME-THOMAS RAYNAL. *Histoire philosophique et politique des établissements et du commerce des Européens dans les deux Indes.* Geneva, 1780.

The Abbé Raynal, one of the leading figures of the French Enlightenment, published the first edition of his 'philosophical and political history' in 1770. In the preparation of the work, he had the assistance of various members of the *philosophe* coteries – notably Diderot, who has been credited with many of the better passages. The result is a violent and somewhat inaccurate attack on the exploitation of natives by Europeans, and in particular on the practice of forcibly converting them to Christianity. The work caused a considerable stir in Europe, and this Geneva edition of 1780 was the first to carry the author's name. The second of the four volumes, shown here, deals with the Spanish and Portuguese conquests in America; the frontispiece is a fanciful representation of Cortes and Montezuma in Mexico. *B.B. 38 Jur.*

2

5. JOSE ANTONIO DE VILLASEÑOR Y SANCHEZ. *Theatro Americano: descripcion general de los reynos y provincias de la Nueva-España.* Mexico, 1746–48.

Villaseñor was a Creole – an American-born Spaniard – who rose through the colonial service to become the official cosmographer for the Kingdom of New Spain. He wrote widely on a variety of subjects: his works include a report on the price of mercury from the Mexican mines, an account of a comet seen over Mexico in 1742, and a poetical panegyric to King Ferdinand VI. The *Theatro Americano*, commissioned by Philip V in 1741, consists of a city-by-city description of New Spain, with statistical accounts of all the Spanish and Indian settlements. It was printed in Mexico in a somewhat old-fashioned style, and the second volume (shown here) was dedicated to Ferdinand VI. *Arch.* Σ 147

6. ANTONIO DE ALCEDO. *Diccionario geográfico-histórico de las Indias Occidentales, ó America: es á saber, de los Reynos del Perú, Nueva España, Tierra Firme, Chile, y Nuevo Reyno de Granada.* Madrid, 1786–89.

Antonio de Alcedo y Bejarano was a Spanish army officer, born at Quito in 1735. He served through the Anglo-Spanish war of 1778–83, notably at the siege of Gibraltar, and attained the rank of colonel. His *Diccionario*, a detailed alphabetical gazetteer of Spanish America, reputedly took him twenty years to compile, and quickly became one of the most-used reference books of the period: an English edition appeared in 1812–15. This particular copy comes from the private library of the Venezuelan revolutionary Francisco de Miranda (see items 26–28), and was acquired in 1828. *233 e. 518*

7. RAFAEL ANTUÑEZ Y ACEVEDO. *Memorias históricas sobre la legislacion y gobierno del comercio de los españoles con sus colonias en las Indias Occidentales.* Madrid, 1797.

Some of the major Bourbon reforms in South America were in the field of trade and commerce: local industries were encouraged, more ports in Spain were opened to the Indies trade, and the colonies were given more opportunity to trade with each other. It was to explain all these changes that Antuñez, a Spanish economist and member of the Consejo de Indias (the governing board for Spanish America), produced his compilation of the relevant legislation. Unfortunately, by the time the work was published Spain was at war with England again, and virtually all contact with the Indies had been lost. *243 e. 91*

8. ANTONIO CAULIN. *Historia coro-graphica natural y evangelica de la Nueva Andalucia*. [Madrid], 1779.

Caulin was a Dominican friar who sailed to the New World as a missionary in 1739, eventually becoming Provincial of his order in the Viceroyalty of New Granada. His book on New Andalusia – the name then given to part of Venezuela and the Guianas – was the result of explorations carried out together with Peter Loefling, a Swedish botanist and disciple of Linnaeus. Loefling died on the expedition, and Caulin's work, though finished in 1759, was not published for another twenty years. The title-page shows an allegorical figure of America surrounded by some of the animals of Venezuela, including a sloth, a tapir and a manatee or sea-cow.

Arch. /70

9. *Mercurio Peruano, de historia, literatura y noticias públicas, que da á luz la Sociedad Académica de Amantes de Lima*. Lima, 1791–95.

The *Mercurio Peruano* is a typical example of some of the locally-based periodicals that appeared in several of the major Spanish American cities in the 1780s and 1790s, symptoms both of the spread of the Enlightenment to America and of the rising tide of local patriotism there. It was published by the Sociedad Académica de Amantes de Lima, and appeared twice a week for five years from 1791, the complete collection consisting of twelve volumes. The articles cover a wide range of topics – politics, literature, economics, archaeology – but the general tendency is as stated in the first issue: 'to make better-known the country in which we live'.

233 e. 225–236

10. ANTONIO PEREZ Y LOPEZ. *Teatro de la legislacion universal de España é Indias, por orden cronológico*. Madrid, 1791–98.

The administrative reforms of the Bourbons and the enlightened despotism of Charles III made great changes to the body of laws in force in Spain and her colonies. Pérez y López, a Seville lawyer, attempted in his 28-volume compilation to reconcile all the various legal codes, civil, canon and local, into one comprehensive sequence. His work provides an alphabetical list of topics, each one with an annotated historical summary of all the legislation currently in force. As with Antuñez' work on the commercial code, the sections covering the Indies were soon overtaken by events: when Spain went to war in 1796 control over her colonies was much weakened, and never fully re-established.

4° A 51 Med. BS.

4

II HUMBOLDT

Friedrich Wilhelm Heinrich Alexander, Freiherr von Humboldt, was born in 1769 in Berlin. From an early age he was determined on the life of a scientific researcher and explorer: before he was thirty he had published a monograph on the vegetation of the mines of Freiberg and made a botanical and geological tour through Switzerland and Italy. In 1799, under Spanish patronage, he set sail for the New World, accompanied by the French botanist Aimé Bonpland. They arrived at Cumaná in Venezuela, and set off to explore the course of the Orinoco river. After a journey of nearly 2000 miles through previously unknown territory they returned to the coast and spent several months on the island of Cuba; then they crossed the South American mainland again on an expedition from Cartagena to Quito, ascending the Magdalena River and crossing the Cordillera of the Andes. From Quito they travelled to Lima and Callao via the headwaters of the Amazon; then by sea to Mexico, where they stayed for a year before returning to Europe.

Humboldt spent much of the next twenty-five years arranging the publication of the mass of scientific, geographical and political information he and Bonpland had collected during their five-year trip. Paris was chosen as the place of publication, and thirty folio and quarto volumes appeared between 1805 and 1834; even so, the work remained incomplete. Humboldt never went back to America (though Bonpland returned to settle in Argentina, and spent several years imprisoned in Paraguay – see item 111). Nonetheless, by his trip and the resulting publications, Humboldt did much to condition the way in which nineteenth-century Europe viewed Latin America.

11. ALEXANDER VON HUMBOLDT. *Voyage aux régions équinoxiales du Nouveau Continent fait en 1799, 1800, 1801, 1802, 1803 et 1804 par Al. de Humboldt et A. Bonpland, rédigé par Alexandre de Humboldt.* Paris, 1814–25.

The publications resulting from the Humboldt-Bonpland expedition fall into three classes: the general narrative, the political essays and the scientific researches. In this the principal narrative account of the trip, Humboldt was determined to produce a report of almost clinical objectivity, rather than a mere 'narrative of personal adventure'. Fortunately the resultant loss in readability was compensated for by the amount and the importance of the information contained in the three volumes – a fourth was planned but never produced – and the work acted as an inspiration to many subsequent nineteenth-century explorers of Latin America.

Hist. a. 39

12. ALEXANDER VON HUMBOLDT. *Vues des Cordillères, et monumens des peuples indigènes de l'Amérique.* Paris, 1810.

This volume, issued as the second atlas supplement to the *Voyage*, is an uneasy combination of mountain views and pre-Columbian art. It contains 69 plates, each with extensive commentary; the plate shown – by far the most spectacular – is a panoramic view of Mount Chimborazo, engraved from Humboldt's own drawing. Humboldt and Bonpland climbed the mountain, which was believed at the time to be the world's highest, in 1802, and the group on the right of the picture may be supposed to represent their party; the figure picking a flower has been held to represent the author himself. *Douce H. Subt. 34*

13. ALEXANDER VON HUMBOLDT. *Essai politique sur le Royaume de la Nouvelle-Espagne.* Paris, 1811.

This is an extremely detailed and highly statistical economic geography of Mexico under Spanish rule. Humboldt was greatly impressed by the enormous mineral resources of the country, and his book led to an upsurge of interest, particularly in England, in the exploitation and development of Mexican silver mines. Companies were floated, speculators were interested, and share prices rose; and when the inevitable crash came in 1830 Humboldt was most annoyed at finding himself held morally responsible for the financial losses. *Mason G. 166, 167*

14. ALEXANDER VON HUMBOLDT. *Essai politique sur l'île de Cuba.* Paris, 1826.

Humboldt had not intended this to appear as a separate work, but an enterprising publisher extracted the chapter on Cuba from the three-volume *Voyage* and issued it as a companion-piece to the essay on New Spain. It caused a certain stir on its appearance as a result of the author's uncompromising attack on the slave-system, which was the mainstay of the island's economy. *243 e. 33,34*

15. ALEXANDER VON HUMBOLDT. *Essai sur la géographie des plantes; accompagné d'un tableau physique des régions équinoxiales. . .* Paris, 1805.

In this seminal scientific work, Humboldt first elaborated the concept of plant geography – the effect of the prevailing climate on the type and pattern of vegetation. He noticed this during his ascent of Mt. Chimborazo, which reaches a height of 20,000 feet above sea level: at different altitudes he found plants typical of tropical, temperate and Arctic climates. His ingenious graphical demonstration of this phenomenon can be seen above (item 147): an elaborate illustration of the mountain's profile, with indications of the locations of the various plants. Humboldt dedicated the German edition of this book to his friend Goethe. *Hist. a. 48*

16. ALEXANDER VON HUMBOLDT. *Personal narrative of travels in the equinoctial regions of the New Continent during the years 1799–1804, by Alexandre de Humboldt and Aimé Bonpland. Translated into English by Helen Maria Williams.* London, 1814–29.

The expedition to America made Humboldt famous throughout Europe, and this translation of the *Voyages* began to appear in London only a few months after the original was published in Paris. The translator was an English poetess and pamphleteer who had resided in France through the Revolutionary and Napoleonic periods; Humboldt himself helped her with the translation, which appeared in seven octavo volumes.

Douce H 210,211

17. ALEXANDER VON HUMBOLDT *Researches concerning the institutions and monuments of the ancient inhabitants of America, with descriptions and views of some of the most striking scenes in the Cordilleras! Translated into English by Helen Maria Williams.* London, 1814.

This translation of the *Vues des Cordillères*, in octavo format with the elements of the title neatly reversed, could hardly present a greater contrast with the folio original (item 12). Only 19 of the 69 plates of the French edition are reproduced: for the other 50 the English reader had to content himself with verbal descriptions. The financial advantages of the smaller format were, however, obvious, and an octavo edition of the French text appeared in Paris two years later. *Douce H 208,209*

18. ALEXANDER VON HUMBOLDT. *Correspondence scientifique et littéraire, recueillie, publiée et précédée d'une notice et d'une introduction par M. de la Roquette.* Paris, 1865.

This first posthumous collection of Humboldt's correspondence contains two contrasting portraits of the great traveller: on the left, a self-portrait at the age of forty-five, drawn from his reflection in a mirror, and on the right a photograph by Friedlander, taken two years before his death at the age of eighty-nine. *210 e. 28*

19. F. DEPONS. *Travels in South America during the years 1801, 1802, 1803 and 1804, containing a description of the Captain-Generalship of Caraccas . . . with a view of the manners and customs of the Spaniards and the native Indians. Translated from the French.* London, 1807.

One of Humboldt's earliest followers was François de Pons, agent for the French government in colonial Caracas. While Pons was in Venezuela he travelled extensively, and on his return to Europe in 1806 published this description of the area. His account of the country is similar to Humboldt's essay on New Spain, which was not to appear for another five years: he analyses the colony systematically, describing its history, geography, population and commercial possibilities. And like Humboldt he was most impressed with the natural resources of South America – 'the new promised land' as he calls it.   *2094 e. 10,11*

III INDEPENDENCE

The movement for the independence of the Spanish colonies in America began in earnest when the French invaded Spain in 1808. King Charles IV was compelled to abdicate, and the crown was given to Joseph Bonaparte, Napoleon's brother. These events presented problems of loyalty in the Spanish Indies; most of the major cities created ruling juntas governing in the name of Charles' son Ferdinand, and temporary self-government encouraged a desire for permanent independence. By the time the Spanish Bourbons were restored in 1814 there were strong patriotic movements in most parts of Spanish America, and despite the military efforts of Ferdinand's government by 1825 the only American colonies left in Spanish hands were the islands of Cuba and Puerto Rico. By contrast, Brazil's transition to independence was comparatively peaceful: Napoleon's invasion had sent the Portuguese royal family scuttling for safety to Rio de Janeiro, and in 1821 Brazil and Portugal became separate monarchies, both ruled by the House of Braganza.

Europeans had a large part to play in these struggles: a British force captured Buenos Aires in 1806 (and was immediately expelled by a French general), British and European merchants bolstered the trade of independent Mexico and Brazil, and Peninsular Spaniards commanded the loyalist armies while mercenaries from many parts of Europe fought under Bolívar and San Martín. The books produced by and about these outsiders, many of which are shown here, provide an unofficial history of the birth of the new nations of America.

20. J. G. STEDMAN. *Narrative of a five years' expedition against the revolted negroes of Surinam*. 2nd edition. London, 1813.

Stedman's book is an instructive indication of the eighteenth-century European attitudes to colonial revolt. A young Englishman of Dutch descent, he volunteered to accompany an expedition sent out from Holland to quell a slave rebellion in Surinam, or Dutch Guiana. In the narrative, first published in 1796, Stedman does not disguise his sympathy with the rebels and his detestation for the cruelties practised by the slave-owners; nevertheless he helped crush the revolt, and ends his book with an improving 'emblematic picture' – drawn by the author and engraved by William Blake – of Europe supported by Africa and America.

20950 d. 4,5

9

21. MARCUS RAINSFORD. *An historical account of the Black Empire of Hayti; comprehending a view of the principal transactions of the revolution of Saint Domingo.* London, 1805.

Rainsford, an Irishman, visited Haiti in 1799; he was imprisoned and sentenced to death, but released by the black leader Toussaint L'Ouverture. He published an account of his adventures in the 'Black Republic' in 1802, under the title *Saint Domingo.* By 1805, however, the situation had changed: French troops had invaded the island to put down the ten-year-old insurrection, and had once again been expelled (though Toussaint had died in a French prison), leaving Haiti under the regime of the self-proclaimed emperor Jean-Jacques Dessalines. Rainsford now attempted this general historical overview of the country, charting its progress from colony to republic to empire.   *23404 d. 10*

22. ALEXANDER GILLESPIE. *Gleanings and remarks collected during many months of residence in Buenos Ayres and within the upper country.* Leeds, 1818.

In 1806 the English admiral Sir Home Popham, fresh from the capture of Cape Town, determined to strike a blow at Spain, at that time allied to Napoleon's France. Without Admiralty approval, he crossed the Atlantic, accompanied by General William Beresford and 1,400 soldiers, and with surprising ease captured Buenos Aires. The Creole population, however, did not take kindly to British occupation: a large ad hoc force assaulted the city under the command of a French officer, Jacques de Liniers, and after three days' fighting Beresford and his men were forced to surrender. Gillespie served on the expedition as a major in the Royal Marines, and recounts in this book his experiences as a prisoner-of-war both in Buenos Aires and in the interior, until his release in 1807.   *8° BS. M. 91*

23. *The trial of Lieutenant General John Whitelocke, commander in chief of the Expedition against Buenos Ayres.* London, 1808.

The news of Beresford's capture of Buenos Aires was received with delight in Britain, and John Whitelocke was appointed to command 8,000 men on a further expedition to Spanish America. He reached the River Plate in July 1807, and succeeded in taking Montevideo. An assault on Buenos Aires, however, met with stubborn resistance, and Whitelocke concluded an agreement with the opposing general by which the attack – and Montevideo – were given up in exchange for the release of British prisoners. This capitulation caused outrage in England, and Whitelocke was court-martialled and cashiered; but the Creole population, who had achieved their success without any aid from the Spanish government, felt a new sense of confidence in their own resources – and a growing dissatisfaction with Spanish rule.   *231 a. 127*

24. *Mémoire general sur le gouvernement de Buenos Ayres.* 1810.

When the French invaded Spain in 1808, Buenos Aires refused to acknowledge the authority of the new government in Madrid, and two years later a provisional junta was appointed to govern the colony independently. The manuscript shown dates from this period; it contains thoughts on the organization of the new state to be created from the old viceroyalty of La Plata, paying particular attention to military preparation and foreign policy. Written in three small notebooks and interleaved with blotting-paper, the manuscript starts with a copy of a letter written to the ruling junta in 1810 by the French renegade general Dumouriez (see item 26); a chronic meddler, he declares his intention of preparing recommendations on the organization of an army for Buenos Aires. So it is possible – but by no means certain – that the manuscript, which reached the Bodleian in obscure circumstances in 1921, is in fact General Dumouriez' own draft of his plan. *MS. French e. 17–19*

25. E. E. VIDAL. *Picturesque illustrations of Buenos Ayres and Monte Video.* London, 1820, reprinted Buenos Aires, MCMIXXX [sic. Really 1943?].

Emeric Essex Vidal, an officer in the Royal Navy, made these drawings of the River Plate in 1817 and 1818, while he was purser of H.M.S. *Hyacinth.* They appeared in London in monthly parts between May and October 1820, each number containing four illustrations. Unfortunately, the Bodleian does not possess a copy of the first edition, but this facsimile, produced and hand-coloured in Germany, gives some idea of the splendour of the original. *2098 b. 6*

26. FRANCISCO DE MIRANDA. *Correspondence du Général Miranda avec le Général Dumourier . . . depuis Janvier 1793.* Paris, [1793].

Miranda, the precursor of Venezuelan independence, was born about 1754. The American War of Independence, in which he served with the French army, made him an advocate of South American independence of Spain. After the French Revolution he went to Paris, hoping for aid in spreading the revolution to America; disappointed in this, he joined the French army again and served in the northern campaigns of 1792–93. When the commander-in-chief, General Dumouriez, declared against the Republic and deserted to the enemy, Miranda too was suspected of treason, and imprisoned despite the publication in this volume of all his correspondence with Dumouriez. Eventually he succeeded in escaping to England, where he continued his own campaign for Latin American independence. *Vet.E 5 e. 362*

11

27. PHILIP, EARL STANHOPE. *Notes of conversations with the Duke of Wellington,
1831–1851*. London, 1888.

While trying to persuade the British government to espouse the cause of
America against Spain, Miranda came into contact several times with the
Duke of Wellington, as is shown in Stanhope's account of the Duke's
table-talk. The British government intended to assemble an army in
Ireland under the command of the Duke – or Sir Arthur Wellesley, as he
then was – for the invasion of Mexico; Miranda wanted the expedition
diverted to Venezuela. In the event, neither project came to maturity:
Napoleon invaded Spain, and Wellesley's army was sent thither to fight
the Peninsular War.   *22873 e. 5*

28.   JAMES BIGGS. *The history of Don Francisco de Miranda's attempt to effect a
revolution in South America*. London, 1809.

Disappointed in both France and England, Miranda decided to start the
revolution at his own expense. With a band of North American volunteers, he made a landing on the Venezuelan coast in 1806. The expedition
was a fiasco. Fifty U.S. citizens were captured by the authorities, and
eight were executed. In this book (first published in Boston in 1808) Biggs,
one of the volunteers, graphically described the sufferings and the lost
opportunities.
   Miranda's hour seemed at last to have come in 1811, when Venezuela
proclaimed a republic; aided by Simón Bolívar, he was given the command of the army. But after an earthquake and a military defeat the
insurrection collapsed: Bolívar escaped, but Miranda was captured, and
died in 1816 in a Spanish prison.   *8° BS. H. 225*

29. H. L. V. DUCOUDRAY-HOLSTEIN. *Memoirs of Simon Bolivar, president-
liberator of the Republic of Colombia*. London, 1830.

Ducoudray-Holstein was a French officer who had served throughout the
Revolutionary and Napoleonic Wars. He joined the Venezuelan patriot
army in 1815, and was appointed chief-of-staff to Bolívar, who was
amassing forces for another invasion of Venezuela. It seems to have been
Ducoudray who first suggested to him that a legion be formed of foreign
volunteers to aid the revolutionary cause; Bolívar immediately saw the
possibilities of the idea, and an agent was sent to London to begin
recruiting. Ducoudray himself, however, did not remain long in the
service: he left after a disagreement in 1816, and fourteen years later
published these critical and rather ill-natured reminiscences of his former
chief.   *30. 126*

30. GUSTAVUS HIPPISLEY. *A narrative of the expedition to the Rivers Orinoco and Apure in South America.* London, 1819.

Hippisley, a half-pay lieutenant of British cavalry, was the first to be recruited in London to the South American patriot cause: he was given the rank of colonel, and the duty of organizing the First Venezuelan Hussars, which he was to command. The regiment was formed, gorgeously apparelled and dispatched to Venezuela; but Hippisley, like Ducoudray, found the reality of service on the Orinoco not at all to his taste, and was soon back in England writing this justification for his defection.

8° BS. N. 80

31. *Recollections of a service of three years during the war-of-extermination in the republics of Venezuela and Colombia, by an officer of the Colombian navy.* London, 1828.

The author of this memoir made his own way to Venezuela in 1818 to join the British Legion fighting there, and accepted a command in the Colombian navy. Though unimpressed by Bolívar's appearance ('so disproportioned that instead of commanding respect he would perhaps, if seen in the common sphere of domestic life, excite risibility') he respected the Liberator's powers of leadership, and remained in the service until after the Battle of Carabobo, when he was awarded Colombian citizenship and a grant of land. His account, written after his return to Europe, gives a vivid picture of the cruelty and brutality of the struggle.

28. 181

32. *The life of Alexander Alexander, written by himself and edited by John Howell.* Edinburgh, 1830.

Alexander, who joined Bolívar's army as a common soldier, gives a more charitable, and rather more credible, view of the Liberator as he appeared to the men under his command, in one of the few accounts we have from the ranks.

30. 4

33. JAMES HACKETT. *Narrative of the expedition which sailed from England in 1817, to join the South American patriots.* London, 1818.

Five regiments were eventually raised in England and sent out to fight for independence in South America. The soldiers of the British Legion provided a valuable stiffening for Bolívar's army, and were to play a decisive part at the Battle of Carabobo, which marked the end of the war in Venezuela; while two of the Liberator's most faithful aides were Daniel Florence O'Leary, an Irishman, and Belford Wilson, an Englishman. The author of this account was not, alas, of that stamp: after sailing with the first volunteers, Hackett defected almost immediately and returned to England to write this criticism of the enterprise.   *8° BS. M. 260*

34. J. H. ROBINSON. *Journal of an expedition 1400 miles up the Orinoco and 300 up the Arauca.* London, 1822.

Robinson was one of the first medical men to put his skill in the service of the patriot cause; he went to Angostura with the British Legion, and was appointed by Bolívar Director-General of Hospitals in the Free Provinces of New Granada. The first campaign on which he served was a laborious expedition up the Orinoco and Arauca rivers; his party was surprised by a Spanish force, and had to retreat, under very difficult conditions, back down the Arauca. Sickened by the dust, the heat and the brutality, Robinson died in Angostura from the effects of the climate, shortly after writing this journal of his experiences.   *Vet. A6 e. 81*

35. *Campaigns and cruises in Venezuela and New Granada and in the Pacific Ocean from 1817 to 1830; also, Tales of Venezuela, illustrative of revolutionary men, manners and incidents.* London, 1831.

The author of this work, generally identified as Richard Longueville Vowell, left England as a volunteer in 1817. He served under Bolívar at Boyacá, the battle that finally liberated New Granada, and under Sucre at Pichincha, which did the same for Quito; then he joined the Chilean service under Lord Cochrane (see item 40) and campaigned energetically along the Pacific coast. All this Vowell narrates in the first of his three volumes, leaving the other two for a pair of short novels of life in Venezuela during the revolution.   -   *31. 291-293*

36. *Fairburn's edition of the speech of Chas. Phillips, Esq., the celebrated orator, to General D'Evereux and the regiments under his command previous to their embarkation at Dublin to join the Spanish patriots in South America.* London, [1819].

In emulation of the British Legion, an Irish Legion was raised in Dublin by John D'Evereux, an Irishman who had lived in the United States since the 1798 rising against England. By the end of 1819 he had assumed the rank of major-general – despite a total lack of military experience – and re-cruited some two thousand men for the cause. The pamphlet shown is an account of the banquet held on 20 July, the night before the embarkation of the first volunteers. The general tone of the speeches can be seen from the extract on the title-page. The reality was less uplifting: when the Irish reached Venezuela (D'Evereux prudently remained in Dublin), they found that no preparation had been made for them. Many of the Legion were eventually expelled from the patriot army for mutiny.   *G. Pamph. 2750*

37. *A statistical, commercial and political description of Venezuela, Trinidad, Margarita and Tobago, from the French of M. Lavaysse.* London, 1820.

Jean-François Dauxion-Lavaysse spent more than fifteen years in the West Indies, first in Haiti, where his family owned land and slaves, and later in Trinidad, where he had fled from the slave insurrection. Back in France he published his *Voyage to Trinidad, Tobago, Margarita and various parts of Venezuela*, the work here transformed by editorial tampering into a handbook for Britons fighting with Bolívar. The editor-translator, Edward Blaquiere, rearranged the contents so as to bring Venezuela to the fore, added an appendix containing extracts from Bolívar's Angostura speech, and wrote an introductory attack on Spanish arrogance and brutality. The resulting volume was dedicated to General D'Evereux of the Irish Legion – who succeeded in serving throughout the wars of independence without taking part in a single battle.   *100. 24 r. 22*

38. *Recuerdos sobre la rebelion de Caracas.* Madrid, 1829.

This book gives one of the comparatively few accounts of Bolívar's revolution seen from the losing side. The author, José Domingo Díaz, was secretary of the loyalist junta in Caracas at the time of the revolts led by Miranda and Bolívar, and one of the leading apologists for the Spanish cause. After the achievement of independence he continued to oppose the new régime, issuing open letters from Puerto Rico (still a Spanish colony) calling upon the Venezuelans to return to their true allegiance. His history of the revolution was published after his return to Spain in 1828.

233 e. 210

39. *Extracto de las providencias expedidas por el Marques de la Concordia, y relacion del estado en que dexa los reinos del Perù, Quito, Chile y Provincias altas de Buenos Ayres en los diez años de su govierno.* 1816

Peru was the most loyal of the Spanish colonies in South America, and in José Fernando de Abascal y Sousa, Marqués de la Concordia, she had the most effective viceroy. Abascal had an instinct for leadership, and reacted to the revolutions with vigour and determination: under his rule Peru became the bastion of Spanish power in the Americas, and Peruvian forces crushed rebellion in Upper Peru (Bolivia), Quito and Chile. When he retired at the age of 73, after ten years of firm government, he left this account of his stewardship. The Bodleian manuscript of the work, acquired in 1860 for the sum of five guineas, is one of the only two known: the other, in Seville, is addressed to Joaquín de la Pezuela, Abascal's successor as viceroy.   *MS. Add. C. 17, 18*

40. THOMAS COCHRANE, EARL OF DUNDONALD. *Narrative of services in the liberation of Chili, Peru and Brazil from Spanish and Portuguese domination.* London, 1859.

In 1817, José de San Martín led an Argentine army across the Andes and succeeded in expelling the Spaniards from Chile. He now determined to make a seaborne attack on the coast of Peru, and to that end appointed a new commander to the Chilean navy – Thomas, Lord Cochrane, afterwards 10th Earl of Dundonald. Cochrane, who had left England under a cloud after a stock exchange scandal, proved himself a commander of genius, and in less than two years the liberation of Peru was accomplished. After a disagreement with Bolívar, he transferred his services to Brazil, where he helped the Emperor Pedro I to break free from Portugal. Cochrane returned to England in 1825, but this account of his South American adventures was not published until the year before his death.

233 e. 117, 118

41. JOHN MILLER. *Memoirs of General Miller in the service of the Republic of Peru.* London, 1828.

Another Briton to join the Chilean forces for the liberation of Peru was William Miller, who had seen service in the Peninsular War and at the disastrous battle of New Orleans. He commanded the marines on Cochrane's flagship, and after the landing in Peru became both a brigadier-general and an intimate of Simón Bolívar. He went on to fill various high military and political offices in Peru: by the time his brother John published these memoirs in London, based on William's letters, journals and recollections, he had already spend some years as govenor of Potosí, and eventually rose to the rank of Grand Marshal.

28. 405, 406

42. JOHN MAWE. *Travels in the interior of Brazil, particularly in the gold and diamond districts of that country, by authority of the Prince Regent of Portugal.* London, 1812.

Brazil had an easier passage to independence than the Spanish-ruled countries of South America. When the French invaded Portugal in 1807, the whole Portuguese royal family fled to Brazil, led by the Prince Regent (who became King John VI in 1816). Rio de Janeiro now became the capital of the Portuguese monarchy, and the court encouraged the opening of the country to foreign – particularly British – traders and entrepreneurs. John Mawe was a naval officer and mineralogist, who had accompanied General Whitelocke to Buenos Aires in 1807 (see item 23). In 1809–12 he made various excursions to the mining areas of Brazil, and his vivid account of the trip enjoyed considerable success in England. The frontispiece represents negro slaves washing the gravelly soil to find diamonds.

2 △. 782

2. Court Day at Rio (item 44)

43. HENRY KOSTER. *Travels in Brazil.* 2nd ed. London, 1817.

Koster, unusually among travellers to Latin America, actually made the trip for the sake of his health: in 1809, finding Spain and Portugal 'not in a state to be visited by an invalid', he decided to take his illness to Pernambuco; and there he remained, apart from a few months in 1811, until 1815. He thus witnessed the country in its transition from a colonial dependency to the centre of a worldwide monarchy, and he was most impressed. He even seriously considered starting a new life as a Brazilian planter, but reluctantly dismissed the idea because of his antipathy to the institution of slavery. The plate exhibited shows the kind of life he might have led: a rich planter and his wife on a journey, he on horseback, she carried in a litter by two slaves and attended by a third.   *2096 e. 46, 47*

44. *Sketches of Portuguese life, manners, costume and character, by A. P. D. G.* London, 1826.

The anonymous author of this account spent many years among the Portuguese, first as a member of the civil service from 1793 to 1804 and later for fifteen years from 1809, when he accompanied Wellington's army. He also evidently made at least one trip to Brazil, as is proved by this striking illustration of a court-day (or Beijamão – 'Kiss-hand') in Rio some time between 1816 and 1821. John VI sits in state, with the Queen and the Crown Prince by his side, and receives the obeisance and the petitions of a long line of dignitaries, ecclesiastical and civil.

In 1821 John at last returned to Lisbon, leaving his son Pedro in Rio as regent. To prevent Brazil's reversion to colonial status, Pedro led a virtually bloodless coup; he broke all links with Portugal, and by the end of 1822 had become Emperor Pedro I of an independent Brazilian Empire.
26. 661

45. HENRY CHAMBERLAIN. *Views and costumes of the city and neighbourhood of Rio de Janeiro, Brazil, from drawings taken by Lieutenant Chamberlain during the years 1819 and 1820.* London, 1822, reprinted Rio de Janeiro, 1943.

Henry Chamberlain was the son of the British consul-general and chargé d'affaires in Rio, whose baronetcy he later inherited. These illustrations were published in London by Ackermann as a companion-volume to Vidal's views of Buenos Aires (item 25). As in that case, the Bodleian seems never to have received its copyright copy of the original, and the volume shown is a later reprint, presented to the Library in 1980. The plate represents a party of newly-imported invalid slaves 'under the care of a Capataz, or Keeper, who generally bears the Badge of his Office – a Whip'. For more about slavery in Brazil, see item 58.   *2096 b. 9*

46. JOSE GUERRA. *Historia de la revolucion de Nueva España, antiguamente Anáhuac; ó Verdadero origen y causas de ella con la relacion de sus proyectos hasta el presente año de 1813.* London, 1813.

The beginnings of independence in Mexico came not from the Creole upper classes but from the Indian peasantry, who rebelled in 1810, led by Miguel Hidalgo, a parish priest. Faced with a social revolution, the Creoles supported the Spanish administration, and by 1815 both Hidalgo and his successor Morelos had been captured and executed. José Servando Teresa de Mier Noriega y Guerra (generally known as Servando Teresa de Mier) was a Mexican preaching friar expelled from New Spain for his freethinking tendencies. After adventures in Spain and France he settled in London, where he became the leading propagandist for the Mexican revolution. In this work he justifies the revolt by quoting Spanish law, and encourages his compatriots to adopt English institutions and political virtues.   *233 e. 212, 213*

47. BASIL HALL. *Extracts from a journal, written on the coasts of Chili, Peru and New Spain, in the years 1820, 1821, 1822.* 3rd edition. Edinburgh, 1824.

When independence finally came to New Spain it was as a conservative reaction to liberalizing tendencies in Madrid. In 1821 Augustín de Itúrbide, the Mexican army commander, declared for independence, and published his *Plan of Iguala*, by which Mexico – on the lines of Brazil – would become a constitutional monarchy under a Bourbon prince. Basil Hall was a Royal Navy officer who held a command in the Pacific coast of America. His journal contains valuable descriptions of the independence struggles in Chile and Peru, and for the third edition Hall expanded his account of the Mexican revolution, which was arousing considerable interest in England. On the pages shown he quotes in full the Treaty of Cordoba, by which the viceroy, Juan O'Donajú, accepted Itúrbide's *Plan of Iguala*. The treaty was, however, subsequently repudiated by the Spanish government.   *24. 576, 577*

48. *A statement of some of the principal events in the public life of Agustin de Iturbide, written by himself.* London, 1824.

After the rejection of his compromise, Itúrbide formed a junta to proclaim Mexican independence in 1821; the following year the first National Congress met, and elected him Emperor Agustín I of Mexico. There was, however, considerable republican opposition, and Itúrbide was forced into exile in 1823. His career was followed with enthusiasm in England, and during his exile the Irish barrister Michael Quin translated his memoirs into English. Quin was a firm supporter of the Emperor, and wrote an introduction pointing out his Anglophile tendencies: 'There can be litle doubt that the restoration of his influence would be attended with particular advantages . . . to the British people'. Itúrbide returned to Mexico in 1824 and was immediately executed. 24. 617

49. JOEL R. POINSETT. *Notes on Mexico made in the Autumn of 1822, accompanied by an historical sketch of the Revolution.* London, 1825.

Poinsett was the influential – and very unpopular – United States Minister to Mexico from 1825 to 1829; this book, however, dates from his first visit to the country in 1822. His fervent liberalism and tireless concern for U.S. interests are already apparent; they were later to lead to his being declared *persona non grata* for his incessant meddling in Mexican internal affairs. His period of diplomatic service left two permanent monuments: the name of the flower Poinsettia, which he imported into the United States, and the Mexican-Spanish word *poinsettismo,* coined to describe his officious and intrusive behaviour. 25. 738

50. LORENZO DE ZAVALA. *Ensayo histórico de las revoluciones de Megico, desde 1808 hasta 1830.* Paris, 1831; New York, 1832.

Zavala was a lifelong supporter of Mexican independence, and a member of the first National Congress; like Mier in 1813 (item 46) he was an admirer of Anglo-Saxon political institutions, and was anxious to see them adopted in his own country. After a short spell as Minister of Finance in 1829, he embarked on an extended tour of Europe and North America, and published this authoritative if tendentious account of the Mexican revolution while he was on his travels – volume one in Paris, volume two in New York. 233 f. 97, 98

51. FRANCIS HALL. *Colombia: its present state . . . and inducements to emigration.* London, 1824.

Hall's book was written, as the title states, to promote emigration from Europe to Colombia; the author had come to America as aide-de-camp to General D'Evereux, but was soon given command of his own corps of engineers. After the war he settled in Bogotá, and later in Quito, where he began publication of the liberal paper *El Quiteño Libre.* His book, dedicated to Jeremy Bentham, encourages his compatriots to join him; though, unlike some propagandists, he does admit that life in Colombia has problems as well as advantages. He and his journalist colleagues were murdered during political disturbances in 1833. 24. 578

52. CHARLES STUART COCHRANE. *Journal of a residence and travels in Colombia during the years 1823 and 1824*. London, 1825.

Charles Cochrane (not to be confused with Lord Dundonald) was one of the many Englishmen who realised the economic and commercial possibilities of the new nations of America. While serving with the Royal Navy in the Caribbean, he concluded that a great deal of money was to be made from the pearl-fisheries of the Colombian coast; he promptly requested two years' leave of absence and travelled to Bogotá with the aim of obtaining the concession. The Colombian government was very liberal in its treatment of foreigners, and though Cochrane missed the pearl-fishing concession, he received the exclusive right to erect factories in northern Venezuela for working sheet copper – another industry he was perfectly prepared to turn his hand to.   25. 400, 401

53. *Letter from Bernardo O'Higgins to General Sir John Doyle, dated 20 August 1829*.

O'Higgins, the son of an Irishman who rose to be viceroy of Peru, became commander-in-chief of the patriot forces in Chile, and, after San Martín's liberation, Supreme Director of the country. He was anxious to encourage emigration from Ireland to the underpopulated south of Chile, and the Bodleian possesses several letters he wrote on the subject to Sir John Doyle, president of the Society for Improving the Condition of the Irish Poor. In the letter shown, O'Higgins expatiates for twenty-four pages on the economic advantages to Ireland of the reduction in surplus population, and concludes: 'I fear you will consider it presumptuous in a *Chileno* to offer an opinion upon a subject so purely British and Irish, but you may be disposed to pardon him when you consider that he is half an Irishman by blood, and almost half an Englishman by education, and one who hopes ere long to see England and Chile united by the strong bonds of natural interest and esteem'.   *MS. North c. 18, ff. 40-51*

54. *Tom Cringle's log*. Edinburgh, 1834.

A less enthusiastic view of Latin American independence is put forward by the hero of this anonymous novel of seafaring life in the West Indies, first published in *Blackwood's Magazine* 1829 to 1833. The author, Michael Scott, spent many years trading in Jamaica, and seems to have written the story partly from his own experiences. The eponymous narrator laments the changes that have so recently come to America, lately so 'prosperous and happy' under Spanish rule: 'The men of mind tell us, that those countries are now going through the *political fermentation*, which by and by will clear, when the sediment will be deposited . . . We shall see. The *scum* as yet is uppermost, and does not seem likely to *subside*, but it may *boil over'*. This violent and vigorous narrative was deservedly one of the most popular books for boys of the last century, and went through numerous editions.   *Lent by M.D.D.*

55. *Pizarro's Flag*

Throughout the three hundred years of Spanish domination in Peru, the battle-standard which accompanied Francisco Pizarro throughout his campaigns against the Inca Empire was preserved in Cuzco, the original Inca capital. When Cuzco fell to the patriot army in December 1824, the leader, Antonio José de Sucre, at once realised the symbolic value of the flag, and offered it to his commander-in-chief, Simón Bolívar. It was sent to Bogotá, where it still remains in the National Museum, a symbol of the downfall of Spanish oppression in the Americas.

Or rather, most of it remains in Bogotá: for on 8 November 1856 a small portion of the standard was removed by the museum director and presented to the British Minister in Colombia, who in turn passed it on to the Earl of Clarendon, Her Majesty's Secretary of State for Foreign Affairs. And when the Clarendon papers were deposited in Oxford in 1949, it came into the keeping of the Bodleian Library – a small, but hardly insignificant, piece of American history.   *MS. Res. f. 13*

IV EARLY TRAVELLERS

It has been reckoned that between 1815 and 1830 the number of travel books on South America to be published reached a peak which was not equalled until after 1850. Independence had opened up Latin America to visitors from all parts of Europe, and travellers of many kinds took advantage of the new freedom: naturalists came to follow in the tracks of Humboldt and Bonpland, entrepreneurs came to set up new industries, mercantile agents came to trade, ordinary travellers came to explore and admire. Diplomats and consular representatives were sent to smooth out their difficulties.

Such was the demand in Europe and North America for information on the new nations, that it was difficult for the returning traveller not to succumb to temptation and immortalize his experiences in print. Good, bad or indifferent, the accounts – *A narrative of four months in Peru, Rough notes of rides across the pampas* and the like – all sold, and some of them sold extremely well. Many of them even deserved their success. In this section we attempt to show a representative selection, all of them dating from between the year of Waterloo and the mid 1830s – the great age of nineteenth-century Latin American travel.

56. MAXIMILIAN, PRINCE OF WIED–NEUWIED. *Reise nach Brasilien in den Jahren 1815 bis 1817.* Frankfurt-am-Main, 1820–22.

Prince Maximilian, the first of the great nineteenth-century German followers of Humboldt, retired from the Prussian army in 1815 with the rank of major-general to devote himself to the study of geography and the natural sciences. Almost immediately he set off to Brazil, and spent nearly two years exploring the great tropical rain-forests. His account of the trip shows a particular interest in the Indian tribes he met with: he includes word-lists of several of their languages and coloured illustrations of their artefacts. Two plates from his atlas volume are shown in the wall-cases (items 144–5), while the engraving exhibited here depicts the Prince's camp on the Cachoeira river, and gives an idea of the conditions under which he had to carry out his explorations.   *2096 d. 29, 30*

57. MARIA GRAHAM. *Journal of a residence in Chile during the year 1822, and a voyage from Chile to Brazil in 1823.* London, 1824.

Maria Graham (or Lady Callcott, as she became after her second marriage) was one of the more intrepid of the lady travellers of the last century. She set off for Brazil in 1821 with her husband, Captain Thomas Graham, and

they spent several months in Rio; then in 1822, while they were on a voyage to Chile, Captain Graham died off Cape Horn. Distressed but undaunted, his widow stayed in Chile for the rest of the year, and subsequently returned via Juan Fernandez and Cape Horn to Brazil, where she remained until October 1823. Throughout her travels Mrs Graham kept a personal diary which she later published in two parts, embellished with engravings from her own sketches, and with appropriate historical introductions and background material. This volume deals with her experiences in Chile, where she met San Martín and O'Higgins, and formed a lasting friendship with Lord Cochrane.

4^0 Jur. R. 56

58. MARIA GRAHAM. *Journal of a voyage to Brazil and residence there during part of the years 1821, 1822, 1823.* London, 1824.

In this volume Mrs Graham published the diaries of her two periods of residence in Brazil, interrupted by the trip to Chile recounted in item 57. In Rio de Janeiro she became closely acquainted with the recently-proclaimed emperor, Dom Pedro I, and was appointed tutor and instructress to his daughter Donna Maria (afterwards Queen of Portugal). The illustration shown represents a slave-market in Pernambuco: though the slave trade was declared illegal throughout the British Empire in 1807, the practice was not outlawed in Brazil until 1830, and sights like this horrified many a European visitor. The practice of slavery itself continued in Brazil until 1888, when its abolition was instrumental in causing the fall of the Empire.

4^0 Jur. R. 55

59. GILBERT FARQUHAR MATHISON. *Narrative of a visit to Brazil, Chile, Peru and the Sandwich Islands during the years 1821 and 1822.* London, 1825.

Mathison sailed to America from Portugal in May 1821, and spent a year travelling in Brazil and on the west coast before setting off again for the South Sea Islands and the Far East. In his book he cast a rather jaundiced eye over the achievements of Latin American civilization, concluding that 'the prospect which South America displays is far less brilliant than the friend of humanity would desire, or than the generality of persons . . . appear willing to believe'. He seems, however, to have been very taken by the costumes worn by Peruvian women, and his plates offer several examples.

25. 641

60. W. BULLOCK. *Six months' residence and travels in Mexico; containing remarks on the present state of New Spain.* London, 1824.

William Bullock was a traveller and antiquarian of some repute, who collected his own museum of curiosities and opened it to the public in Piccadilly. He set out for Mexico late in 1822 in search of more antiquities to exhibit, and was greatly encouraged in his researches by the Mexican authorities, who actually presented him with a silver mine. On his return to England, laden with curiosities, he opened a new gallery entitled Modern Mexico, and published this narrative of his travels with illustrations drawn by his son. From his account, he seems to have been an earnest admirer of Humboldt, with whose experiences he delights to compare his own. *20890 e. 73*

61. JOHN MIERS. *Travels in Chile and La Plata, including accounts respecting the geography, geology, statistics, government, finances, agriculture, manners and customs, and the mining operations in Chile.* London, 1826.

In 1818 Miers was invited to Chile by Lord Cochrane, with a view to developing the copper and other mineral resources of the country; he accordingly sailed for Buenos Aires with his young bride, and reached the west coast via the pampas and the cordilleras. Miers remained in South America until 1838 (apart from a few months in London in 1825, arranging for the publication of this book) and was responsible for setting up national mints in both Buenos Aires and Rio de Janeiro. His *Travels*, one of the most vivid accounts of nineteenth-century South America, describes in detail the economic and social conditions in Chile and the River Plate states; the drawings shown, both by the author, illustrate the use of lasso and bolas by the pampas Indians. *26. 797, 798*

62. EDMOND TEMPLE. *Travels in various parts of Peru, including a year's residence in Potosi.* London, 1830.

Temple, a rich and rather spoilt young man, contrived to obtain a secretarial post with the Potosí, La Paz and Peruvian Mining Association, one of the many English speculative ventures of the 1820s. He left England for Bolivia in 1825, travelling across the pampas from Buenos Aires, and remained in Potosí with the company until its collapse in 1826. Temple blamed the company's failure on the shareholders, and published this scathing narrative of his experiences three years after his return to England. *30. 769*

63. H. G. WARD.*Mexico*. 2nd edition. London, 1829.

As his title-page proclaims, Sir Henry Ward was British chargé d'affaires in Mexico from 1827 to 1829. The book, originally published in 1828 under the title *Mexico in 1827*, is an account of independent Mexico for the English reader, in two parts: the first volume describes the political and economic state of the country, while volume two (not shown here) is a relation of Sir Henry's travels, mainly in the mining districts. Lady Ward drew the view from the window of the British Consulate in Mexico City engraved as the frontispiece. Sir Henry Ward died in 1860, as Governor-General of Ceylon. *20890 d. 104*

64. ALCIDE D'ORBIGNY. *Voyage pittoresque dans les deux Amériques.* Paris, 1836.

Orbigny was a French palaeontologist, who spent seven years in North and South America on behalf of the Paris Museum of Natural History. In addition to a nine-volume scientific report, *Voyage dans l'Amérique Méridionale* (1835–37), he published this popular account of his travels, including summaries of previous explorations of the continent. The frontispiece is designed to leave no doubt in the reader's mind as to the author's importance for the history of America: he is ranked with Columbus, William Penn, and Alexander von Humboldt.   *Vet. E6 d. 2*

65. JOHANN MORITZ RUGENDAS. *Voyage pittoresque dans le Brésil, traduit de l'Allemand par M. de Golbery.* Paris, 1835.

Rugendas was a member of a family of Bavarian painters, and in the course of his life travelled – and painted – extensively in Latin America. In 1821 he accompanied Georg Heinrich von Langsdorff, a German who acted as Russian consul-general in Rio, on his excursions through Brazil, and this volume is the result. Rugendas took great care over the preparation of the book, even travelling to Paris to see it safely through the press; it consists of 100 engravings, depicting the landscapes of the country and the manners and costumes of the inhabitants, Creole, Indian, and Negro, each with accompanying narrative. The plate exhibited shows the costumes of the Bahia area: the hunter in the boat seems to be trying to sell the dead caiman to the booted and spurred, though rather effeminate, priest.
                                                                          2096 a. 1

66. SIR WOODBINE PARISH. *Buenos Ayres and the provinces of the Rio de la Plata.* London, 1838.

While Ward was British representative in Mexico (item 63), Parish was filling the same office in Buenos Aires, where he signed the first treaty between a European power and one of the new states of America – the Anglo-Argentine treaty of 1825. He left the River Plate in 1832, and six years later published this description of the country: in it, he treats not only the history and geography of the provinces, but gives an account of the geology, and of some of the fossil monsters which had recently come to light there. The frontispiece shows the skeleton of the glyptodon, or giant armadillo.   *38.831*

V HISTORIANS AND SCHOLARS

The systematic study of the history of South America in non-Hispanic Europe can be dated from 1777, the year of the publication of Robertson's *History of America*. Europeans began to take a scholarly interest in the area, Humboldt explored and published his researches, men like William Bullock (item 60) brought back pre-Columbian curiosities, and the movement was under way that was to lead in the 1840s to the classic works of Prescott and the foundation of the Hakluyt Society. Not all the scholarship was disinterested — Lord Kingsborough was determined to prove that the ancient Mexicans were Jews — but much of it is still valuable, with the Hakluyt Society, and Prescott's popularity, lasting into our own day.

67. WILLIAM ROBERTSON. *The history of America*. London, 1777.

Robertson, a Scottish clergyman and 'the first historian of the present age' according to Edward Gibbon, prepared this two-volume *History of America* as a by-product of his *History of the Emperor Charles V*. Despite its general title, it covers the history only of the Spanish settlements in the New World from 1492 down to about 1550: a planned continuation on North America was abandoned because of the War of Independence, and Robertson never seems to have considered Brazil or the West Indies. The work was an immediate success, and on the strength of it Robertson was made a corresponding member of the Royal Academy of History in Madrid. It was the first scholarly modern history of Latin America, and for fifty years was regarded as the last word on the subject.

FF 16-17 Jur. Subt.

68. ROBERT SOUTHEY. *History of Brazil*. London, 1810–19.

In 1795, at the age of twenty-one, Southey went to stay in Portugal with his uncle the Rev. Herbert Hill, who had long been a resident of Lisbon. The young poet was fascinated by the country, and returned to England determined to write its history, using his uncle's extensive collection of Portuguese historical manuscripts. The only part of the projected work ever to appear, however, was this *History of Brazil*; it took ten years to produce, and by the time all three volumes had been published Southey was poet laureate. The work is important not only as the first modern history of Portuguese America but also for its treatment of adjacent areas, such as Paraguay – whose history Southey was later to use as the subject for verse (item 108).

4° *BS. 777-779*

69. LORD KINGSBOROUGH. *Antiquities of Mexico: comprising fac-similes of ancient Mexican paintings and hieroglyphics, preserved in . . . libraries of Paris, Berlin and Dresden . . . Vienna, the Vatican, Rome, Bologna and Oxford; the whole illustrated by many valuable inedited manuscripts. The drawings, on stone, by A. Aglio.* London, 1830–48.

Edward King, Viscount Kingsborough, was stimulated by the sight of a Mexican manuscript in the Bodleian to devote himself to the study of Mexican antiquities, and this set of books was his life's work. He developed the theory that the original inhabitants of the country were the lost tribes of Israel, and decided to prove this by publishing facsimiles of all the pre-Columbian manuscripts then known. To locate the manuscripts he availed himself of the help of the irascible bibliophile Sir Thomas Phillipps; to reproduce them he employed the émigré Italian artist Augustine Aglio; and in 1830 the first volumes appeared, with copious notes by Kingsborough himself. The cost, however, was very high: Kingsborough spent upwards of £32,000 on production costs, and these expenses helped to drive him to a debtor's prison in Dublin, where he died in 1837. The *Antiquities* themselves continued to appear until 1848, when nine of the projected ten volumes were completed. The Bodleian copy is one of only four printed on vellum with the plates coloured and the whole splendidly bound in leather; the plate exhibited reproduces the famous first leaf of the Mendoza Codex. *Mexican Case*

70. *Holograph letters of Kingsborough and Aglio*

Among the letters of Sir Thomas Phillipps in the Bodleian are several from both Lord Kingsborough and his artist Aglio. Shown are: first, a letter from Kingsborough dated 'Monday morning' [1830?] inviting Sir Thomas to come and inspect 'a splendidly bound copy of the Antiquities of Mexico'; and, secondly, a note from Aglio dated 31 May 1830 charging Phillipps £168 for a copy of the *Antiquities*. Subsequent letters in the collection suggest that Sir Thomas took an unacceptably long time to settle this account. *MS. Phillipps-Robinson c. 428, ff. 7-9 (Aglio)*
MS. Phillipps-Robinson c. 621, ff. 113 (Kingsborough)

71. WILLIAM H. PRESCOTT. *History of the Conquest of Mexico, with a preliminary view of the ancient Mexican civilization, and the life of the conqueror Hernando Cortés.* London, 1843.

William Hickling Prescott, the New England historian, did more than any other nineteenth-century writer to introduce English-speaking readers to the wonders of the ancient civilizations of America. This two-volume history of Cortes' conquest of the Aztecs historically marks a great advance on the books by Robertson and Southey: Prescott had access to a far wider range of sources, including material in the Archivo General de Indias in Seville and, of course, Kingsborough's magnificent collection of Mexican codices. The work, and its successor dealing with Pizarro's conquest of Peru, made Prescott famous not only in the U.S. and Britain but throughout Europe and the Hispanic world; and did much to stimulate further research into Latin American history. 43. 1490, 1491

72. *The observations of Sir Richard Hawkins, Knt., in his voyage into the South Sea in the year 1593, edited by C. R. Drinkwater Bethune.* London, 1847.

This was the very first publication of the Hakluyt Society, established in 1846 with the object of publishing the original narratives of important voyages and expeditions, together with other major geographical records. The influence of the Society can be seen from the composition of its Council: Sir Roderick Murchison, president of the Geographical Society, Darwin, Dean Milman and Monckton Milnes, as well as Dr Beke the explorer of Ethiopia, Sir Henry Ellis the librarian of the British Museum and John Forster, Dickens' biographer. Of the 300 or so volumes issued by the Society since its foundation, a large proportion has been concerned with the exploration and conquest of Latin America.
Soc. 2031 d. 4 (1)

73. CLEMENTS R. MARKHAM. *Cuzco: a journey to the ancient capital of Peru; and, Lima: a visit to the capital and provinces of modern Peru.* London, 1856.

Sir Clements Markham, who subsequently was to edit no less than twenty volumes of early travels for the Hakluyt Society, made his own first trip to Peru in 1852, after a visit to W. H. Prescott in Boston. His account of his expedition is divided into two sections: a description of Cuzco and a discussion of the Inca civilization are counterpointed by a visit to Lima and his ideas on modern Peruvian society. In later life Markham became one of the leading British geographers of his generation, president both of the Hakluyt Society and the Royal Geographical Society; Latin American history and politics never lost their fascination for him, and he remained, as the *Dictionary of National Biography* notes, an enthusiast rather than a scholar. 203 b. 239

VI NATURALISTS

Humboldt and Bonpland were by no means the first non-Iberian Europeans to make Latin America their field of exploration, as we have seen from the expedition of La Condamine and others (items 1, 3) and Loefling's trip to the Orinoco (item 8). Nevertheless, the opening-up of the area in the early nineteenth century provided major opportunities for European naturalists, opportunities that were quickly taken. As in many other fields, Humboldt was among the first: his findings on plant geography appeared in 1805, his observations on zoology and anatomy in 1811 and the specimens of the new plants he and Bonpland discovered were published from 1815. Other naturalists followed him to the Americas: Prince Maximilian of Wied went to Brazil in 1815 (item 54, 144–5), Spix and Martius two years later (items 75–77). On the Amazon vast tracts of virgin forest offered to zoologists and botanists the prospect of innumerable unrecorded animal and plant species, while in the 1820s and '30s Patagonia began to yield up skeletons of fossil monsters for the study of geologists and palaeontologists. It was left to Darwin, who had surveyed the coasts of Chile and the Argentine, and Alfred Russel Wallace, who had hunted insects in the Brazilian rain-forests, to provide an interpretation of the new data in their theory of natural selection, first promulgated in 1858.

74. FELIX DE AZARA. *Apuntamientos para la histories natural de los páxaros del Paragüay y Rio de la Plata.* Madrid, 1802–05

Azara was one of the first to attempt a systematic listing of South American species, during his twenty years as a commissioner for delimiting the boundary between Spanish and Portuguese America. Finding himself at a loose end in Paraguay, he determined to make a scientific collection of the local fauna, but soon discovered that the climate made it impossible to keep stuffed specimens for any length of time. At last he decided to content himself with a listing of birds, each one described in detail and collated with Buffon's *Histoire naturelle des oiseaux* (1770–83). The three volumes he prepared and published on the birds of Paraguay and the River Plate contain a total of 448 species.   *189975 e. 14*

75. J. B. VON SPIX & C. F. P. VON MARTIUS. *Travels in Brazil in the years 1817-1820, undertaken by command of His Majesty the King of Bavaria.* London, 1824.

In 1817 Caroline, Archduchess of Austria, sailed to Rio de Janeiro in order to marry Pedro, then Crown Prince of Portugal and later Emperor of Brazil. With the bridal party travelled two scientists from the Academy of Sciences in Munich, with a commission from Maximilian I of Bavaria to carry out a scientific exploration of Brazil. Johann Baptist von Spix, a zoologist, and Carl Friedrich Philipp von Martius, a botanist, travelled widely for three years, making their way from Rio to Pará and up the Amazon to Alto Amazonas. The first edition of their account of the expedition appeared in Munich between 1823 and 1831, and aroused such interest in Britain that this translation of the first two volumes by H. E. Lloyd was published soon after in London.   *24. 720*

76. J. B. VON SPIX. *Avium species novae quas in itinere per Brasiliam annis MDCCCXVII-MDCCCXX . . .* collegit et descripsit J. B. de Spix. Munich, 1824.

Spix and Martius brought so many specimens back from their Brazilian expedition that a new gallery was opened in the Munich museum to hold them all. They were recorded in print in Latin – still the language of international scholarship – throughout the 1820s, with Spix preparing volumes on the new species of reptiles discovered – frogs, lizards, tortoises – in addition to this finely-illustrated collection of previously unknown birds. The illustration shown is of the blue macaw *Anodorynchus maximiliani*, named in honour of the King of Bavaria. Spix died in 1826, and Martius edited several subsequent collections of his zoological specimens.   *1896174 b. 1*

77. C. F. P. VON MARTIUS. *Nova genera et species plantarum quas in itinere annis MDCCCXVII — MDCCCXX per Brasiliam . . . collegit et descripsit C. F. P. de Martius.* Munich, 1823–32.

While Spix was preparing the zoological volumes, Martius concentrated on the production of this comprehensive collection of all the new specimens of plants he had collected on his Brazilian journey. Perhaps more than any other botanist, Martius set his mark on the study of Brazilian plant life: as well as the three volumes of this work he produced books on the country's ferns and palms, and began the monumental *Flora Brasiliensis*, which was not completed until 1906, thirty-eight years after his death. He also found time to write copiously on the Brazilian Indian tribes and their languages, particularly the Tupí.   *19178 c. 4*

78. *Narrative of the surveying voyages of His Majesty's Ships Adventure and Beagle, between the years 1826 and 1836, describing their examination of the Southern shores of South America, and the Beagle's circumnavigation of the globe*. London, 1839.

There can be little doubt that scientifically the most significant expedition to Latin America in the nineteenth century was that which carried Charles Darwin to Patagonia, Chile and the Galapagos, and gave him the evidence on which he formulated his theory of evolution. The voyage of H.M.S. *Beagle* between 1831 and 1836 was officially an Admiralty coastal survey under the command of Robert FitzRoy, carrying the young Darwin as naturalist. It was the *Beagle's* second surveying trip to South America: between 1826 and 1830 she had accompanied another ship, the *Adventure*, under the general command of P. Parker King. Captain FitzRoy published this account of both expeditions in 1839; volume two, with a fine frontispiece, consists of FitzRoy's own narrative of the 1831–36 voyage, while volume three contains Darwin's journal, later published separately as *The Voyage of the Beagle*. Also shown is the general chart of the second voyage, issued with a volume of appendices, and in the wall-case a map of South America prepared from the information brought back by the *Adventure* and the *Beagle*.   *39. 1089–1092*

79. *The zoology of the voyage of H.M.S. Beagle, under the command of Captain FitzRoy, during the years 1832 to 1836; edited and superintended by Charles Darwin*. London, 1840-43.

Darwin returned from his voyage in October 1836 with a large number of specimens, geological, zoological and fossil. With the aid of a grant of £1,000 from the Treasury, he eventually succeeded in publishing descriptions and illustrations of the collection in five volumes; the specimens themselves were presented to various museums. Each volume was prepared, under Darwin's general editorship, by a specialist in the field it covered: the fossil mammals by Sir Richard Owen, the living mammals by George Waterhouse, the birds by John Gould, the fishes by Leonard Jenyns and the reptiles by Thomas Bell. The plate shown is from Waterhouse's volume, and depicts two species of mouse.   *18933 c. 5, 6*

80. CHARLES DARWIN. *Geological observations on South America*. London, 1846.

Darwin had trained as a geologist before he embarked on H.M.S. *Beagle*, and on his return he filled the post of Secretary of the Geological Society from 1838 to 1841. It was natural that after the publication of his journal and the preparation of the zoological records of the trip, he should settle down to write three geological monographs, all resulting from observations made during the voyage. The first dealt with coral reefs, the second with volcanic islands, and the third, shown here, contained general remarks on the geological formations of South America. *18896 d. 2*

81. WILLIAM SWAINSON. *A selection of the birds of Brazil and Mexico.* London, 1841.

Swainson was an accomplished but underrated naturalist and ornithologist of the early nineteenth century. He visited Brazil as early as 1816, in company with Henry Koster (item 43), though the birds he collected there did not appear in book form until 1834 and 1841. Swainson's writings on ornithology were to a large extent vitiated by his acceptance of the quinary system of classification invented by W. S. Macleay and later discredited, but his drawings combine accuracy with artistic skill in a way almost unrivalled in his time. The plates shown are of the Ruby-topaz hummingbird. *1896174 d. 2*

82. ROBERT H. SCHOMBURGK. *Twelve views in the interior of Guiana from drawings executed by Charles Bentley after sketches taken during the expedition carried on in the years 1835 to 1839, with descriptive letter-press by Robert H. Schomburgk.* London, 1841.

Sir Robert Schomburgk was another in the line of great German explorer-scientists and followers of Humboldt. In 1834 the Royal Geographical Society decided to send an expedition to explore British Guiana, and Schomburgk was entrusted with the task. Between 1835 and 1839, with two companions, he explored the Guianan rivers, following the Essequibo and the Rupununi through to the Rio Negro and eventually to the headwaters of the Orinoco. In the course of the expedition they discovered the giant water-lily which they named the Victoria Regia in honour of the new queen. This spectacular volume was published shortly after Schomburgk's return to England, with pictures elaborated from sketches by John Morrison, the expedition's artist. The plate shown is a view of the Ataraipa, a natural pyramid on the Guidaru river. *535. 11t. 5*

83. ROBERT H. SCHOMBURGK. *The natural history of the fishes of Guiana.* Edinburgh, 1841–43.

Schomburgk's explorations in Guiana were carried out almost entirely along the great rivers of the country, and he was most impressed both by the varieties of fish he encountered and by the methods the Indians had of catching them. Soon after his return he published this monograph, with illustrations after drawings made on the spot by the author himself. By the time the book appeared Schomburgk was back in Guiana, where the government had commissioned him to survey the boundary between the colony and Venezuela (long after known as 'the Schomburgk line'); he was knighted on his return to England in 1844. *1895 3 e. 52, 54*

•

84. *Expédition dans les parties centrales de l'Amérique de Sud, de Rio de Janeiro à Lima, et de Lima au Pará, exécutée pendant les années 1843 à 1847, sous la direction du comte Francis de Castelnau*. Paris, 1850–59.

Castelnau's expedition to Latin America set out, sponsored and equipped by the French government, in 1843. Starting from Rio, they crossed without mishap through Paraguay and Bolivia to Peru. On the return journey, however, they were dogged by ill-luck: their guides deserted them, one of the party was killed, and many of their scientific records destroyed, by hostile Indians, and by the time they had descended the Amazon to Pará Castelnau and his companions were more dead than alive. When they reached France they found that their sponsoring government had been overthrown by the 1848 revolution and that there seemed to be no chance of their findings being published. At last their report appeared under the Second Empire in 21 volumes; it contains some fine ornithological plates, including this one showing two species of para- keet. *203 a. 265; 1909 c. 1*

85. CLAUDIO GAY. *Historia física y politica de Chile*. Paris, 1844–71.

Claude Gay was a young French botanist who was commissioned in 1830 by the Chilean government to carry out a thorough scientific survey of the country, and to produce a detailed description of its geography, geology and natural history. For eleven years he travelled through Chile, province by province; in 1839 he was presuaded to add a political history of the Chilean people to his plans. At length, and despite marital problems, all his material was collected, and Gay returned to France in 1842 to arrange for publication. The – by now monumental – work finally appeared, in thirty volumes, and the author was rewarded with Chilean nationality. In addition to maps and botanical drawings, his atlas-volumes contain plates, many of them coloured, depicting Chilean manners and customs: the one shown features a *Chingana*, a type of impromptu open-air fes- tivity. *2343 e. 16; Mason G. 177*

86. ALFRED RUSSEL WALLACE. *A narrative of travels on the Amazon and Rio Negro, with an account of native tribes and observations on the climate, geology and natural history of the Amazon valley*. London, 1853.

Wallace, the co-discoverer with Darwin of the theory of natural selection, set out for the Amazon in 1848 at the age of 25, in company with H. W. Bates. Neither of them had any money, but they hoped to collect ento- mological specimens which they could sell on their return to defray expenses. They parted company in 1850; Wallace continued travelling along the Rio Negro and the Orinoco until 1852, deeply impressed by the majesty of the tropical forests and the splendour of the birds and butterflies. On his return to England, he published this account of his expedition; unfortunately all his specimens had been lost in a shipboard fire.

203 a. 246

87. HENRY WALTER BATES. *The naturalist on the River Amazons.* London, 1863.

Bates was 23 when he and Wallace set off on their scientific exploration of the Amazon. When they parted company, Bates continued his route upriver, spending a total of eleven years in Brazil and collecting no less than 8,000 species of insect new to science. When he returned to England, his health seriously affected, he published this narrative of his travels at the instigation of Charles Darwin; it has been called 'one of the most delightful books of travel in the English language'. The frontispiece shows an incident which happened to Bates near Ega on the upper Amazon: he found hemself mobbed by a crowd of curl-crested toucans after shooting one of their number.

203 c. 222, 223

88. RICHARD SPRUCE. *Notes of a botanist on the Amazon & Andes, edited and condensed by Alfred Russel Wallace.* London, 1908.

While Bates and Wallace were collecting insects on the Amazon, Spruce was there on behalf of a syndicate of British botanists, sending them back specimens. In all he spent some fifteen years in northern Brazil, Peru and Ecuador, collecting more than 7,000 species of flowering plants alone, in addition to ferns, mosses, lichens and fungi. In 1864 he returned to England with his health shattered and all his savings lost by fraud. Because of his illness, he was unable to publish the details of his researches, and it was not until fifteen years after his death that his friend Wallace collected and edited his notes for the press.

19179 e. 6

VII MEXICO AND THE MEXICAN EMPIRE

One of the more disastrous cases of European meddling in Latin American affairs was Napoleon III's attempt to set up a Mexican Empire under French protection. Since independence, Mexico had suffered severely from internal contentions, and had lost more than half her national territory to the U.S. in the war of 1846–48. In 1861 France determined to intervene, ostensibly to enforce the payment of foreign debts. With the support (soon withdrawn) of Spain and Great Britain, a French force landed at Veracruz, marched on Mexico City and set up a puppet government. Ignoring Benito Juárez, the liberal president, who had withdrawn northwards with his government, Napoleon found a suitable European prince to act as head of state: Archduke Ferdinand Maximilian of Habsburg, a well-meaning young man, too tolerant in his opinions for the clerical and reactionary elements who were supposed to support him. He was installed by French arms in 1864. When Napoleon announced in 1866 that the French forces were to withdraw, the Emperor saw his Empire collapse around him. Maximilian was taken prisoner, tried by court-martial and executed by firing-squad.

89. C. NEBEL. *Voyage pittoresque et archéologique dans la partie la plus intéressante du Mexique.* Paris, 1836.

Nebel was a French architect who spent five years in Mexico, measuring and sketching the Aztec and Toltec monuments. His *Voyage pittoresque* was originally intended to be accompanied by a narrative volume entitled *Anahuac*; it contains views of Mexico and illustrations of pre-Columbian artefacts very much in the style of Humboldt's *Vues des Cordillères* – and Humboldt himself provides a commendatory introduction. But Nebel also includes pictures of everyday life in Mexico in the 1830s, and it is for these that his book is principally known. The plate shown illustrates contemporary costume in Mexico City, and the facing text gives us the artist's views on Mexican womanhood. *Mason Z. 238*

90. *Life in Mexico, during a residence of two years in that country, by Madame C___ de la B___, with a preface by W. H. Prescott.* London, 1843.

The authoress of this popular volume was Fanny Calderon de la Barca, née Inglis, the Scottish wife of the first Spanish envoy to independent Mexico. Her letters give a clear-eyed and somewhat ironical account of the political upheavals of the Santa Anna period. As the wife of the Spanish minister, she delights to make unfavourable comparisons between the current state of the country and the idyllic, departed days of viceregal rule.   *203 e. 373*

91. MAXIMILIAN, EMPEROR OF MEXICO. *Recollections of my life.* London, 1868.

Maximilian of Habsburg, certainly one of the most unfortunate of European visitors to Latin America in the nineteenth century, was prevailed upon to accept the crown of Mexico in 1863, and in June 1864, accompanied by his wife and empress, Charlotte of Belgium, he made a triumphant entry into Mexico City to begin his short reign. It was not his first visit to South America; these *Recollections* recount, among other excursions, a botanical expedition he made to the tropical forests of Brazil in the 1850s. Regrettably, the memoirs only deal with his life from 1851 to 1860, and make no reference at all to his Mexican Empire.   *203 f. 133-135*

92. *Boletin de las leyes del Imperio Mexicano, ó sea Código de la Restauracion; coleccion completa de las leyes, publicado por José Sebastian Segura.* Mexico, 1863–65.

This collection of laws and decrees issued by the French-backed Provisional Government, and later by the Imperial Government itself, started publication before Maximilian's arrival in Mexico, and ceased long before his downfall. The introduction reads oddly today, with its certainty of a New Order, stable and lasting, thanks to the 'magnanimous intervention of H.M. the Emperor of the French'.   *2338 e. 137*

93. *Letter from P. Campbell Scarlett, British minister in Mexico, to the Foreign Secretary, Lord Clarendon, dated 10 May 1866.*

Peter Campbell Scarlett was the British envoy accredited to Maximilian's court in 1864; many of his dispatches are in the Bodleian among the papers of the fourth Earl of Clarendon, three times Foreign Secretary between 1853 and 1870. In this letter Scarlett passes on to the British Government a request from the Emperor for a good portrait of Queen Victoria 'for whom he entertained the most sincere regard and affection'. On the previous letter, dated 29 March, can be seen the ominous superscription 'Instability of the Empire – Unpopularity of the French'. Scarlett was one of those

4. The Firing Squad, 1867 (item 95)

who, after the withdrawal of the French troops, advised Maximilian not to abdicate, and must therefore bear some responsibility for his eventual fate.   *MS. Clar. Dep. c. 102, f. 138.*

94. FELIX, PRINCE OF SALM-SALM. *My diary in Mexico in 1867, including the last days of the Emperor Maximilian, with leaves from the diary of the Princess Salm-Salm.* London, 1868.

Prince Felix zu Salm-Salm was a Prussian cavalry officer who volunteered to fight for the Federal Army in the American Civil War. He came to Mexico in 1866, to become Maximilian's aide-de-camp and his last and truest friend. He was with the Emperor when he was captured by the republican army in May 1867, and shared his imprisonment. Salm and his young American wife, a former circus-artiste, tried to arrange for Maximilian's escape, but to no avail; Princess Salm even went to Juárez himself to plead for the Emperor's life. Her pleadings were ignored: Maximilian faced a firing-squad on 19 June 1867.   *233 f. 67, 68*

95. PERCY F. MARTIN. *Maximilian in Mexico: the story of the French Intervention (1861-1867).* London, 1914.

This history of the Mexican Empire contains a rare photograph of the members of the republican army who formed the firing-squad for Maximilian's execution. One of the party, Aurelio Blanquet, later rose to the rank of general and himself faced a firing-squad under Pancho Villa. In his pocket was found the 20-peso gold piece given to him by the Emperor in 1867.   *2338 d. 6*

96. PEDRO PRUNEDA. *Historia de la Guerra de Méjico desde 1861 á 1867 con todos los documentos diplomáticos justificativos.* Madrid, 1867.

This history appeared in Spain only a few months after Maximilian's death, the first and one of the best of the European accounts of the French intervention in Mexico. Pruneda was a Spanish liberal; while he sympathised with Maximilian (who is described and illustrated on the pages shown) he admired Juárez' dedication to the cause of liberty, and believed that Mexico should keep herself free of foreign entanglements.
                                                          2338 c. 14

97. *Maximilian: a tragedy.* Dublin, 1868.

The dramatic possibilities of Maximilian's tragic story were soon recognized, and the ill-fated Mexican Empire has provided the background for many novels and films of our own century. This anonymous tragedy (with 'any profits devoted to the Ragged Boys' Home of Dublin') seems to have been the first attempt to dramatize the story. The author adds love-interest: Juárez is portrayed as being in love with one of the Empress' ladies-in-waiting, and treacherously offers the Emperor's life in return for her favours. In the opening scene, Juárez serenades his lady-love offstage, to the sound of a guitar.

Malone e. 318 (11)

VIII LATER TRAVELLERS

With a few exceptions, the accounts of later nineteenth-century travellers in South America lack much of the interest of their predecessors of the 1820s. The experience of travel was to some extent devalued, and travel-literature followed: growing prosperity made it possible for more people to make the trip, steam-ships made the crossing quicker and easier, and the increase in literacy meant that there were more and more at home anxious to read of their experiences. In addition, the work of observing and recording nature in South America was rapidly being completed, or so it appeared. The only field of research still expanding was that of ethnology and anthropology: from about the 1890s an explorer found on the upper Amazon would be more likely to be observing the Indian tribes, as did Whiffen and Koch-Grünberg, than to be collecting beetles or ferns, as did Bates or Spruce.

We try to present here a reasonable cross-section of travellers in Latin America from the 1850s to the First World War; our selection includes two French explorers of the old school, two British mountaineers, an orchid-hunter and a man who would be king.

98. O.-A. DE TOUNENS. *Orllie-Antoine Ier, Roi d'Araucanie et de Patagonie: son avénement au trône et sa captivité au Chili.* Paris, 1863.

The French attempt to found an empire in Mexico had been presaged in the previous decade in the farcical efforts of Orélie-Antoine de Tounens to become King of Araucania and Patagonia. Tounens, a French adventurer, decided to take advantage of the constant state of warfare between the fierce Araucanian Indians of southern Chile and the Santiago govern-ment; he sailed to South America, and posing as the Indians' protector against the Chileans persuaded them to accept him as their king. Unfor-tunately, his kingdom existed only on paper: the Araucanians would not fight for him, and the authorities simply locked him up and sent him home to France, where this impressive justification appeared four years later.   *2343 d. 1415*

99. THOMAS WOODBINE HINCHLIFF. *South American sketches; or, A visit to Rio de Janeiro, the Organ Mountains, La Plata and the Paranà.* London, 1863.

Hinchliff was a barrister and a founder-member of the Alpine Club who did much to popularise the sport of mountaineering. After injuring his arm in the Alps, making it impossible for him to attempt any more difficult climbs, he took to travel: this book recounts his experiences in Brazil and on the pampas of Uruguay and Argentina. He seems to have had to the full that impatience with the actions of foreigners so common in the nineteenth-century English traveller: he regards the Argentine civil war of 1861, which prevented his trip to the cordilleras, principally as a matter for amusement. *203 c. 232*

100. LOUIS & ELIZABETH AGASSIZ. *A journey in Brazil.* London, 1868.

Jean Louis Rodolphe Agassiz, the noted Swiss naturalist and geologist, had first come into contact with Brazil in 1826, when he was invited by Martius to help in the arrangement of Spix' collection of fishes after the latter's death (see item 76). After a life devoted to ichthyology and geology, Agassiz at last visited Brazil for himself from his new home in the United States, at the age of 58. With his wife, he stayed for a short time in Rio, then ascended the Amazon to the Peruvian border. This account of the trip was mainly the work of Mrs Agassiz; it was first published in Boston in 1867, and went through many editions in the U.S. and Europe. *2096 d. 25*

101. PAUL MARCOY. *A journey across South America.* London, 1873.

Paul Marcoy, whose real name was Laurent Saint-Cricq, crossed from the coast of Peru to the Atlantic via the Andes and the Amazon. His principal scientific interest, insofar as he had one, seems to have been ethnology: he spent much time among the Indian tribes of the upper Amazon, and his sketches have been skilfully elaborated by his illustrators, Koch and Riou. In the words of his translator, Elihu Rich, 'M. Marcoy is, *au fond*, and always, the ARTIST, in search of materials for his pencil; and the student of humanity, observant of all that was new and piquant in social life and character'. *Hist. a. 75*

102. JAMES MUDIE SPENCE. *The land of Bolivar; or, War, peace and adventure in the land of Venezuela.* London, 1878.

Like Hinchliff, Spence was an enthusiastic member of the Alpine Club, and for him the culmination of his visit to Venezuela seems to have been his ascent of Mount Naiguatá, near Caracas. Apart from the mountains, he cultivates a rather flippant attitude to the country he is visiting: referring to the general ignorance of Venezuela, he says that 'the capital was only known to most Englishmen by the advertisement of "Fry's Caracas Cocoa", whilst a British minister once accredited there is said to have spent two years in a vain search for his destination'. *203 e. 520, 521*

103. J. CREVAUX. *Voyages dans l'Amérique du Sud.* Paris, 1883.

A French doctor and naval officer, Jules Crevaux explored extensively in the Guianas, Venezuela and the Andes between 1876 and 1881; he was eventually killed by Toba Indians while on an expedition to the Pilcomayo river in 1882. Like Marcoy, he was very fortunate in his illustrator, Edouard Riou, who is perhaps best known for his illustrations for Jules Verne's *Voyages Extraordinaires* which were appearing about this time. In the plate shown, Dr Crevaux is plying his theodolite while his Guianan negro servants relax beside him. *2092 c. 6*

104. ALBERT MILLICAN. *Travels and adventures of an orchid-hunter.* London, 1891.

Millican was a fervent orchid-collector of a type that became increasingly common as the craze for orchids spread through Europe towards the end of the last century. Between 1887 and 1891 he made five trips to the orchid-growing areas of Colombia and the West Indies, and this volume contains a cheerful account of some of his experiences. While he was on another orchid-hunting trip in 1899 Millican was killed in an affray in a small village in Colombia. *2093 e. 2*

105. THOMAS WHIFFEN. *The North-West Amazons: notes of some months spent among Cannibal tribes.* London, 1915.

Whiffen was a cavalry officer on the retired list who was inspired by a reading of A. R. Wallace's *Travels on the Amazon* (item 86) 'to go somewhere and see something of a comparatively unknown and unrecorded corner of the world'. To this end he set off for Brazil in April 1908, and spent several months travelling in the region of the Putumayo and the upper Amazon. He started by making a vain search for the French explorer Eugène Robuchon, who had disappeared in the area in 1906 (a disappearance attributed by some to the activities of Arana's rubber company – see section XI); but Whiffen soon became fascinated by Indian tribes he came into contact with, and his book is full of photographs of them, sketches of their artefacts and word-lists of their languages. *247238 d. 3*

106. THEODOR KOCH-GRÜNBERG. *Vom Roraima zum Orinoco: Ergebnisse einer Reise in Nordbrasilien und Venezuela in den Jahren 1911–1913.* Berlin, 1916-28.

One of the foremost German ethnologists of his generation, Koch-Grünberg typifies the more detailed, systematic process of anthropological investigation. He made three trips to South America in the course of his career to investigate Indian tribes: in 1898–99 he was on the Xingu river, in 1903-05 in north-west Brazil and in 1911–13 in the mountain-regions of Guiana and Venezuela. It was on this last trip that he collected material for the work shown, a five-volume account of the Indians living between Mount Roraima and the Orinoco river. The frontispiece illustrates Koch-Grünberg at work, gathering material from a native informant. *247235 d. 3*

IX PARAGUAY AT PEACE AND WAR

From 1864 to 1870 a war of unusual intensity was fought in South America, when the small, land-locked republic of Paraguay resisted the Triple Alliance of Brazil, Argentina and Uruguay. Paraguay had always been regarded as the most mysterious of American nations. Under Spanish rule the Jesuits established there model Indian communities — the famous Reductions, which Cunninghame-Graham was to call 'a vanished Arcadia'. After the departure of both Jesuits and Spaniards, Paraguay fell under the rule of the despotic isolationist José Gaspar Rodríguez de Francia, and the tradition of autocracy was continued under his successors Carlos Antonio López and Francisco Solano López. The War of the Triple Alliance was eclipsed in the European public mind by other world events – the U.S. Civil War, the Spanish revolution, the Franco-Prussian War, not to mention the French intervention in Mexico, all happened in the same decade. But there were many Britons and Americans involved in Paraguay, both as combatants and as observers, and their accounts, which began to be published in the late 1860s, contain valuable material on the history of the war.

107. MARTIN DOBRIZHOFFER. *Historia de Abiponibus, equestri bellicosaque Paraquariae natione*. Vienna, 1784.

One of the first Europeans to write about Paraguay was Father Dobrizhoffer, an Austrian Jesuit who was in the country as a missionary from 1749 to 1767. The first of the Jesuit communities was founded in Paraguay in 1610. Their aim was not only to christianize the Indians, but to help them live a more comfortable mode of life by encouraging them to grow their own food and to live together in amity. Dobrizhoffer, however, carried out most of his missionary labours among the fierce 'wild Indians' of the Chaco, hitherto resistant to Christianity; it was here that he came into contact with the Abipones whom he describes in this charming and discursive book. An edition in English appeared in 1822, at the instigation of Robert Southey.   *2345 e. 53-55*

108. ROBERT SOUTHEY. *A tale of Paraguay*. London, 1825.

Southey had read deeply on the subject of Paraguay in the preparation of his *History of Brazil* (item 68); an incident narrated in Father Dobrizhoffer's work on the Abipones remained in his mind, and formed the basis of this verse-tale, one of the laureate's better works. The story concerns a young Indian convert's foreknowledge of his own death, and Dobrizhoffer himself appears as one of the characters. 25.242

109. J. P. & W. P. ROBERTSON. *Letters on Paraguay, comprising an account of a four year residence in that republic, under the government of the dictator Francia.* London, 1838.

John Parish Robertson was one of the many British merchants who attempted to open up the new nations of America to European trade. In 1811, after spending three years as a clerk in Rio de Janeiro, he went as a mercantile agent to Asunción, capital of the newly-independent Paraguay; he was apparently the first Briton ever to penetrate there. In Asunción he and his brother William (who joined him in 1813) witnessed the ascent to power of the fanatically isolationist Dr Francia, who became dictator in 1814 and expelled the Robertsons, with many other foreign traders, in 1815. More than twenty years later the brothers published this account of their time in Paraguay; originally advertised as being in two volumes, their work soon acquired a third, with the rather more startling title of *Francia's Reign of Terror*. Francia himself remained in sole control of Paraguay until his death in 1840. *8° F. 385–387 BS.*

110. J. R. RENGGER & M. LONGCHAMP. *Essai historique sur la Révolution du Paraguay, et le gouvernement dictatorial du docteur Francia.* Paris, 1827.

Rengger and Longchamp, both Swiss medical men, sailed to America in 1818 with the intention, shared by so many at the time, of making a scientific exploration of some part of the interior. Unfortunately for their plans, they chose to visit Paraguay, still virtually unknown to the outside world. They reached Asunción in July 1819, and found it under the control of the despotic Dr Francia; refused permission to leave the country, they had to remain there until 1825. During their period of detention, Rengger and Longchamp were forced to witness Francia's persecution of the elite of the old colonial society, and give a graphic account of it in their book, which seems to have been written entirely by Rengger. 2345 e. 230

111. J. R. RENGGER & M. LONGCHAMP. *The reign of Doctor Joseph Gaspard Roderick de Francia in Paraguay; being an account of a six years' residence in that republic, from 1819 to 1825. Translated.* London, 1827.

This translation of Rengger's narrative appeared in London shortly after the publication of the first edition. It is open at the account of Rengger's interview with Dr Francia on the subject of the arrest and detention of Aimé Bonpland, Humboldt's erstwhile companion. Bonpland, while carrying out a botanical investigation on the Paraná river in 1821, came into contact with Paraguayan troops who attacked and arrested his party on suspicion of spying. He was forcibly detained in Paraguay for ten years.   27. 673

112. GEORGE THOMPSON. *The war in Paraguay, with a historical sketch of the country and its people, and notes upon the military engineering of the war.* London, 1869.

On Good Friday 13 April 1865, the forces of President Francisco Solano López invaded the Argentine province of Corrientes. It was the start of the War of the Triple Alliance, which was not to end until López himself had perished on the field of battle, and close on a million Paraguayans were dead – virtually the entire male population of the country. One of the president's most trusted commanders in the war was Colonel George Thompson, a former British Army officer who became a specialist in fortifications and entrenchment. Thompson remained in the Paraguayan service until he was captured by the allied powers in 1868; by the time he came to publish this narrative of his experiences he had turned violently against his former chief.   233 f. 76

113. CANDIDO LOPEZ. *A Campanha do Paraguai, de Corrientes a Curupaiti, vista pelo Tenente Cándido López.* Rio de Janeiro, 1973.

Cándido López, a young painter from Buenos Aires, joined the Argentine forces on the outbreak of war. He witnessed the first fifteen months of the war proper from July 1865; but at the Battle of Curupaytí in September 1866 he lost his right arm. Laboriously re-educating himself to paint with his left hand, he spent the next twenty years producing a large collection of detailed and accurate oil-paintings of scenes and battles at which he had been present. Two of them are shown here, the crossing of the Rio Corrientes and the encampment at Uruguayana, from a luxurious set of reproductions made in Brazil in 1973; two more are exhibited elsewhere (items 149–50).   2345 a. 3

114. THOMAS J. HUTCHINSON. *The Paraná, with incidents of the Paraguayan War and South American recollections, from 1861 to 1868.* London, 1868.

Hutchinson was the British Consul in Rosario, and a great advocate of British emigration to the River Plate area. The work shown here is principally an account of the historical development of the Argentine provinces (rehashed to a large extent from his 1865 book *Buenos Ayres and Argentine gleanings*), but it does include some vivid descriptions of incidents from the Paraguayan War which the author witnessed.   233 e. 162

115. GEORGE FREDERICK MASTERMAN. *Seven eventful years in Paraguay: a narrative of personal experience among the Paraguayans.* London, 1869.

Masterman was in the service of the Paraguayan government as chief military apothecary from 1861 to 1868. His book contains reminiscences of pre-war life in Asunción and of medical experiences during the war itself; it also shows Masterman to have been a confirmed opponent of President Solano López. In 1868 he was arrested and accused of plotting against the president; despite an attempt to grant him diplomatic status he was imprisoned and, according to his own account, tortured. At length he was released and expelled from the country, and returned to London to write this book. *2345 e. 476*

116. RICHARD F. BURTON. *Letters from the battle-fields of Paraguay.* London, 1870.

Sir Richard Burton, the indefatigable English orientalist and explorer, twice visited the seat of the Paraguayan War, in 1868 and 1869. In writing this book, his aim was to cut through the propaganda produced by both sides and tell the truth about the Paraguayan situation; the result, seen more than a century later, seems to present a far more favourable view of President López and his actions than most of the other accounts that have come down to us. *203 e. 181*

117. CHARLES A. WASHBURN. *The history of Paraguay, with notes of personal observations and reminiscences of diplomacy under difficulties.* Boston, 1871.

Washburn, the U.S. minister in Paraguay from 1861 to 1868, cherished a violent antipathy for President López, a fact that he makes no attempt to hide in his book. The first of the two volumes takes his history down to 1861, leaving all of the second for his memories of life in Asunción before and during the war. Not surprisingly, the American legation was suspected in 1868 of being the centre of the anti-López conspiracy (for which Masterman was arrested), and Washburn was expelled. Unlike Masterman, Washburn was wise enough to delay the publication of his memoirs until the war was over, thus giving himself the satisfaction of describing in his final chapter 'Lopez, dying, left no Friend to mourn him – His Name universally accursed – The Character of López not to be judged by any Human Standard – A Mental and Moral Deformity.' *2345 d. 313*

X *NOSTROMO* AND ITS SOURCES

Joseph Conrad's Costaguana is the most complete creation of a Latin American republic by an imagination writing in English. Professor Norman Sherry, in *Conrad's Western world* (Cambridge University Press, 1971) has identified the sources on which Conrad drew to supplement his own short and, by the time of *Nostromo*, remote experiences of South America – the 1876 voyage of the *St. Antoine* to Venezuela, Colombia and the West Indies, his second voyage outside European waters. Costaguana is a composite republic – there are elements in it from the River Plate, from Paraguay, Chile, Colombia and Venezuela and Panama, and some of these can be found in the accounts here exhibited. Conrad's Polish and Catholic origins, as well as his imagination, saved him from the Anglo-Saxon prejudices many of them contain.

Other works used by Conrad and shown in this exhibition are Masterman (item 115), Burton (item 116), Washburn (item 117).

118. JOSEPH CONRAD. *Nostromo: a tale of the seaboard*. London, 1904.

' . . . a damned bad name; the book ought to have been called Costaguana'. – R. B. Cunninghame Graham in a letter to Edward Garnett.

2561 e. 2829

119. ANTON GOERING. *Venezuela de hace un siglo: cuadros de Anton Goering*. Caracas, 1969.

This painting by the German naturalist and artist Anton Goering (1836–1905) shows the victorious *amarillo* army of Antonio Guzmán Blanco in 1870. The soldiers have yellow cockades, the colour of Guzmán's liberal party. It is the sort of military gathering Conrad might have seen in his short stay in Venezuela. *1700876 c. 8*

120. FREDERICK BENTON WILLIAMS. *On many seas: the life and exploits of a Yankee sailor*. London, 1897.

This 'plain story of a plain man' contains the episode of the stolen lighter of silver that became in Conrad's mind the seed of *Nostromo*. He had heard the same story, he writes in the Author's Note, 'in 1875 or '6, when very young . . . somewhere on the Tierra Firme seaboard during the troubles of a revolution'. The book is open here at the anecdote. Conrad had found *On many seas*, 'a shabby volume picked up outside a second-hand bookshop', a quarter of a century after his West Indian voyage.   *23136 e. 27*

121. EDWARD B. EASTWICK. *Venezuela: or, Sketches of life in a South American republic; with the history of the loan of 1864.* London, 1868.

Eastwick went to Venezuela in June 1864 on financial business, for the generous fee of one thousand pounds for three months and all expenses paid. His account is both pompous and lively: 'The first time I went to a tailor . . . he came in with the inevitable cigar in his mouth . . . walked straight up to me, shook hands and asked me how I did. He then sat down on the counter, put various questions to me regarding my coming to Venezuela, talked on general subjects and at the end of about a quarter of an hour intimated that he was ready to oblige me if I wanted a coat. This tailor was an officer of rank in the army. . .' Eastwick was used to more deference out East. Conrad draws on his description of the city of Valencia.   *203 e. 101*

122. S. PEREZ TRIANA. *Down the Orinoco in a canoe.* London, 1902.

Conrad was introduced to the Colombian writer, diplomat and business-man Santiago Pérez Triana, by his friend R. B. Cunninghame Graham, who here introduces the English version of Pérez Triana's account of his 1893 journey into voluntary exile, first published in Spanish in Paris, 1897. Conrad confessed to using Pérez Triana as his model for Don José Avellanos, elder statesman of Costaguana, author of *History of Fifty Years of Misrule*, Minister to the Courts of England and Spain etc. etc. A Liberal and an anti-imperialist, Pérez Triana contributed the chapter on modern Latin America to the original *Cambridge Modern History*. The quotation on the title page of *Down the Orinoco* is from the black Colombian poet Candelario Obeso (1849–1884), an early exponent of poetry in popular language and theme.   *2094 e. 4*

123. CHARLES DANIEL DANCE. *Recollections of four years in Venezuela.* London, 1876.

Dance was 'a Mission Priest in the diocese of Guayana.' Conrad used his description of Venezuelan affairs in the fifties, and borrowed particularly the name and character of General Sotillo.   *203 f. 530*

124. RICHARD ARTHUR SEYMOUR. *Pioneering in the Pampas, or The first four years of a settler's experience in the La Plata camps*. London, 1869.

Seymour's description of the Italian *fonda* and its owner at Frayle Muerto, Argentina, was the model for the Costaguanan inn and its keeper, the old Garibaldino Giorgio Viola. Seymour was a more reflective writer than, say, Eastwick: 'It is curious how cosmopolitan one gets living in any part of the New World . . . Some of one's British prejudices are removed and some strengthened; one feels confirmed in the first article of a Briton's creed, that there is no place like England, and no people like Englishmen, but one feels also that other nations possess kind feelings and warmth of heart . . . This, I must add, does *not* include the Indians'.   *203 f. 238*

125. JOSEPH CONRAD. *Gaspar Ruiz: the story of a Guerilla chief*. In *The Pall Mall Magazine*, Vol. 38. London, 1906.

Conrad's Chilean story *Gaspar Ruiz* was inspired by the history of a certain Benavides recorded in the journal of Captain Basil Hall, R. N., (item 47), with elaborations from the *Memoirs of General Miller* (item 41), and Charles Darwin (item 78).   *Per. 2705 d. 24*

XI THE PUTUMAYO RUBBER SCANDAL

Roger Casement, whose reputation had first been made as an investigator in the Congo, was consul-general in Rio de Janeiro when appointed by Sir Edward Grey in July 1910 to form part of a commission to enquire into the conduct of the Peruvian Amazon Company. Accusations against the company for maltreatment of Indians were first made by the American Walter Hardenburg, and these were substantiated and enlarged in Casement's report, finally published in July 1912. The affairs of the company were made the subject of a House of Commons Select Committee, and Casement, now knighted, gave generous assistance to the Anti-Slavery and Aborigines' Protection Society in their presentation to the Committee. His correspondence with the Society's officers, with other material on the Amazon rubber industry, is in the Society's papers in Rhodes House Library.

The Peruvian Amazon Rubber Company Ltd. was registered in London in 1907, the successor of the Peruvian firm Julio C. Arana Hermanos. In 1908 it dropped the word 'Rubber' from its title. The Company had English and Peruvian directors; its management was controlled by Julio César Arana. Both he and his enterprise survived the scandal with little material damage – rubber gathering on a large scale on the Amazon basin was ultimately ended by Malayan competition.

126. *La Felpa*. Año 1 – Núm. 3. Iquitos, Peru, 30 September 1907.

This paper was published in opposition to Julio C. Arana by one Benjamin Saldaña Rocca. It and its successor *La Sanción* contain many accusations later the subject of Casement's inquiries. Opposition to Arana seems to have been the main motive for the papers' existence. This collection comes from the papers of the Anti-Slavery and Aborigines' Protection Society, in Rhodes House Library. *N. 2343 b. 10*

127. W. E. HARDENBURG. *The Putumayo: the devil's paradise*. London, 1912.

The first revelations of atrocities committed against the Indians by rubber-gatherers in the Upper Amazon that succeeded in affecting English opinion were those made by Walter Hardenburg, a young American engineer, about the activities of Julio César Arana's Peruvian Amazon Company. Hardenburg travelled down the Putumayo from Colombia in 1907–8, and published an account of his observations and sufferings in the magazine *Truth* in 1909. *2343 e. 39*

128. *Roger Casement's report to the Foreign Secretary, Sir Edward Grey, dated 17 March 1911.*

Casement's report is a model of detailed investigation carried out under difficult conditions. *MS. Brit. Emp. s. 22 G. 317*

129. PETER SINGLETON-GATES & MAURICE GIRODIAS. *The Black Diaries: an account of Roger Casement's life and times with a collection of his diaries and public writing.* Paris, 1959.

The 1959 publication of Casement's *Black Diaries* by Peter Singleton-Gates, former Fleet Street journalist who had been given copies in 1922, and Maurice Girodias, proprietor of the Olympia Press, forced the Home Office to grant access to the originals. The government's use of the diaries after Casement's conviction for treason in 1916 had led *The Times* to declare 'We cannot help protesting against certain other attempts which have been made to use the press for the purpose of raising issues which are utterly damaging to Casement's character but which have no connection whatever with the charges on which he was tried'. The reader of 1980 will find it hard to see why these pedestrian records with their occasional homosexual notes were ever called 'Black'.

The Black Diaries prints Casement's report and his 1910 Putumayo diary on facing pages. *Arch. D. d. 45*

130. *A letter of Sir Roger Casement to Charles Roberts, M.P. Las Palmas, Canary Islands, 27 January 1913.*

Charles Roberts was Chairman of the House of Commons Select Committee on the affairs of the Peruvian Amazon Company. Casement writes sending his diary: 'I had it with me, but have not read it for 2½ years! It is often almost unintelligible – altho' *I* can read it all. Naturally there is in it something I should not wish anyone to see – but then it is as it stands . . . The value of the thing, if it has any value, is that it is sincere and was written with (obviously) never a thought of being shown to others but for myself alone – as a sort of *aide memoire* and mental justification and safety valve . . . There is much, as you will see in my diary, would expose me to ridicule were it read by unkind eyes. . .'. *MS. Brit. Emp. s. 22 G. 344*

XII HUDSON

William Henry Hudson was born at Quilmes near Buenos Aires in 1841, the child of American parents of English ancestry. His childhood – described in *Far away and long ago* – was an idyllic one. At 24, an experienced field naturalist, he was collecting bird-skins for the Smithsonian Institution; he wrote letters on Argentine bird-life which were published in the *Proceedings* of the Zoological Society of London. At the age of 33 he sailed for England where he was to remain until his death in 1922. Success did not come easily to him in London: his first two books, both novels, were failures, and he began to make his name only in the 1890s with his reminiscences of nature-watching in Patagonia and La Plata, and with his books on British birds. From about the turn of the century his works began to enjoy a wider popularity: *Green mansions*, his most successful novel, appeared in 1904, and *Far away and long ago* in 1918, four years before his death. Approximately half of Hudson's literary output was concerned with Latin America.

131. W. H. HUDSON. *On the birds of the Rio Negro of Patagonia*. In *Proceedings* of the Zoological Society of London, 16 April 1872.

This was Hudson's first full-length article in the Zoological Society's *Proceedings*, though the journal had already published several of his letters and some classified lists of birds. It was the first of eleven articles Hudson was to contribute, and commemorates the fulfilment of one of his deepest ambitions: to discover a hitherto unknown species of bird. On his trip to Patagonia in 1871 he collected specimens of a species of tyrant-bird which was later found to be unrecorded; P. L. Sclater, his collaborator, named it in his honour *Cnipolegus hudsoni*. A colour-picture of the bird, by J. Smit, accompanied the article. Hudson and Sclater later collected their joint contributions to the Zoological Society's *Proceedings* and published them in two volumes as *Argentine ornithology* (1888–89). Per. 18933 d. 124

132. W. H. HUDSON. *The purple land that England lost: travels and adventures in the Banda Oriental*. London, 1885.

This was Hudson's first and best novel – a picaresque account of the adventures of a susceptible young Englishman journeying through the Banda Oriental. The work was not at first well received: one reviewer found it 'a farrago of indecent nonsense and lies.' Nineteen years later, however, the work was reissued in London, and the American edition of

1916 has an introduction by no less a person than Theodore Roosevelt. The purple land of the title is Uruguay, purpled by the blood spilt during the post-independence decades of war and insurrection; it was lost to England as a result of the abortive 1807 invasion (item 23).

256 e. 1702, 1703

133. W. H. HUDSON. *The naturalist in La Plata*. London, 1892.

After the failure of *The purple land* and of his second novel, Hudson turned again to his career as a naturalist. He collected his articles on Argentine ornithology, and followed them up with two volumes based on his experiences in the pampas. This was the first of them, and also the first of his works to bring him some success: it was highly praised by A. R. Wallace, among others. It is not a personal narrative (though it becomes very discursive at times) but a vivid description of the desert pampas and the wild life that makes its home there. The illustrations are by J. Smit, the artist who painted *Cnipolegus hudsoni* for the Zoological Society in 1872. *189975 e. 1*

134. W. H. HUDSON. *Idle days in Patagonia*. London, 1893.

The second of Hudson's ornithological reminiscences, this book tells of the expedition to Patagonia, whose findings provided the material for his first published article, shortly before his voyage to England. His adventures included a narrow escape from shipwreck. Again the illustrations are by J. Smit, although some plates are by Alfred Harvey. *189975 d. 2*

135. W. H. HUDSON. *El Ombú*. London, 1902.

This was Hudson's second attempt to write stories recalled from his life in the pampas, and was dedicated to his friend R. B. Cunninghame Graham. The ombú is a native Argentine tree. In the title-story of this collection, it watches over the decline of a house and the ruin of the families who inhabit it. Hudson's birthplace in Quilmes was known as 'The House of the Twenty-Five Ombús'. *2561 e. 866*

136. W. H. HUDSON. *Green mansions: a romance of the tropical forest*. London, 1904.

Hudson's best known work, *Green mansions* was his last full-length novel. The story of Rima, the strange forest-spirit, half woman and half bird, brought Hudson more readers than ever before, and ensured that in future his books would bring him a steady income. The author himself, however, had a low opinion of this, as of his other prose romances: 'The story doesn't move – it simmers placidly away'. *2561 e. 2223*

137. W. H. HUDSON. *Far away and long ago: a history of my early life*. London, 1918.

Hudson had been living in England for nearly forty-five years when he published this account of his childhood on the plains of Argentina. His memories, however, were as vivid as ever, and this evocative narrative has generally been regarded as his best work. He never revisited the pampas, and feared that much of the bird population had been destroyed by the increase in immigration – particularly Italian immigration – to the River Plate. *1893 e. 33*

138. W. H. HUDSON. *Birds of La Plata; with twenty-two coloured illustrations by H. Gronvold*. London, 1920.

As has been previously noted, Hudson's contributions to the *Proceedings* of the Zoological Society were collected and published in 1888–89 as *Argentine ornithology*, though the first name on the title-page was that of his editor and annotator P. L. Sclater. Hudson always felt that his love of birds was of a different kind from that of his fellow-ornithologists: it was the living bird which mattered to him, not the expertly-stuffed and neatly-classified museum specimen. He therefore decided to republish his contributions to the earlier work, excluding Sclater's notes, with coloured plates by the distinguished bird-artist H. Gronvold. The result is a fit companion for *The naturalist in La Plata* and *Far away and long ago*: a description, in non-technical language, of the two hundred or so Argentine birds that the author knew best. *1896175 d. 2*

139. R. B. CUNNINGHAME GRAHAM. *The Ipané*. London, 1899.

This is the earliest collection of the graceful sketches of the versatile Cunninghame Graham, author, traveller, pioneer socialist and Scottish Nationalist. He had visited Paraguay shortly after the disastrous War of the Triple Alliance, and retained his affection for Spanish America throughout his long and varied life. *The Ipané* contains incidents from Paraguay, Argentina and the Texas borderlands, the famous anti-imperialist essay 'Niggers', and, from this stretch of the Thames Valley, his account of William Morris's funeral at Kelmscott. *24712 e. 46*

140. A. F. TSCHIFFELY. *Don Roberto; being the account of the life and works of R.B. Cunninghame Graham, 1852-1936.* London, 1937.

The photograph of Cunninghame Graham shown here was taken while he was writing to Morley Roberts (Hudson's first biographer) the letter placed opposite, dated 28 February 1936, from Hudson's birthplace, the House of the Twenty-Five Ombús. He died in Buenos Aires less than a month later, on 20 March.

The house, the ombú trees, their descendants and the birds are still there, in the keeping of the Hudson Society of Argentina. *2112 e. 145*

MAPS AND PICTURES

141. The Compleat Explorer: the French botanist Edouard André sets off on his journey through Colombia, 1875. From *American pintoresca.* Barcelona, 1884. *2092 c. 5*

142. South America, from original documents including the survey by the officers of H.M. Ships *Adventure* and *Beagle,* by John Arrowsmith. From *narrative of the surveying voyages of His Majesty's Ships Adventure and Beagle.* Vol. 1. London, 1839. See item 78. *39. 1089*

143. South America, with its several divisions according to the possessions of the European powers, by Thomas Kitchin. London, 1794.
(E) H 1 (151)

144. Puri Indians in their hut (plate 3).
145. Excursion up a tributary of the Rio Doce (plate 5). Both from MAXIMILIAN, PRINCE OF WIED-NEUWIED. *Reise nach Brasilien in den Jahren 1815 bis 1817: Kupfer und Karte.* Frankfurt-am-Main, 1820. See item 56.
2096 a. 6

146. Carte du Mexique et des pays limitrophes situés au Nord et à l'Est, dressée d'après la grande carte de la Nouvelle-Espagne de M. Al. de Humboldt . . par J. B. Poirson, 1811. From ALEXANDER VON HUMBOLDT. *Atlas géographique et physique de la Nouvelle-Espagne.* Paris, 1811.
20890 a. 2

147. Géographie des plantes equinoxiales: tableau physique des Andes et pays voisins. From ALEXANDER VON HUMBOLDT. *Essai sur la Géographie des plantes.* Paris, 1805. See item 15. *Hist. a. 48*

148. School room map of South America, by the Scottish School Book Association, drawn and engraved by J. Gellatly. Edinburgh, n.d.
This map, dating from the 1840s, is surprisingly inaccurate for school-

room use, particularly as to the international boundaries. Colombia, Venezuela and Ecuador are shown as one country, though they had in fact been separate states since 1830, and Patagonia seems to be regarded as a country independent of both Chile and the Argentine – a state of affairs prevailing only in the dreams of Orélie-Antoine de Tounens (see item 98).   H 1. 111

149. Surrender of Uruguaiana, 18 September 1865, by Cándido López.
150. Brazilian Field-Hospital at Paso de la Patria, 17 July 1866, by Cándido López. Both from the collection of plates illustrating the Paraguayan War, referred to at item 113.   *Lent by M.D.D*